Listen to Me

Listen to Me

THE STORY OF ELIZABETH QUINN

ELIZABETH QUINN
AND MICHAEL OWEN

Michael Joseph
LONDON

First published in Great Britain by Michael Joseph Ltd
44 Bedford Square, London WC1
1984

© 1984 Elizabeth Quinn and Michael Owen

British Library Cataloguing in Publication Data

Quinn, Elizabeth
Listen to me: the story of Elizabeth Quinn.
1. Quinn, Elizabeth   2. Actresses — United
States — Biography
I. Title   II. Owen, Michael
792'.028'0924   PN2287.Q/

ISBN 0 7181 2288 7

Typeset by Alacrity Phototypesetters,
Banwell Castle, Avon. Printed and bound
in Great Britain by Billing & Sons Limited,
Worcester.

Contents

Acknowledgements   vi
List of Illustrations   vii
Prologue   ix
Chapter   1   London 1981   1
Chapter   2   Childhood   14
Chapter   3   Schooldays   24
Chapter   4   Family Life   41
Chapter   5   College   58
Chapter   6   The Turning Point   74
Chapter   7   Chicago   88
Chapter   8   Spectrum, Texas   104
Chapter   9   Los Angeles   123
Chapter   10   New York   137
Chapter   11   London   161
Chapter   12   A Long Run   180
Epilogue   205

Acknowledgements

The extract from *Children of a Lesser God* is published courtesy of Mark Medoff and Westmark Productions Inc. (© 1980 by Westmark Productions Inc., All Rights Reserved). Michael Owen would like to thank all those who contributed to this book, including Gordon Davidson, Trevor Eve, Jean Worth, Anita Quinn, Billy Quinn, Philipa Ailion, Bob Steinberg, Manny Azenberg, Rena Down, Frank Marino, Clarence Russell, Richard Gibbe, Phyllis Kasha, James Sheldon, the unknown author of the poem on p. 95 and, above all, Joan Pritchett.

List of Illustrations

between pages 52 and 53
Aged five
London headlines
Elizabeth and Billy
Jack and Anita
Mrs Dunn's classroom
Thirty years on

between pages 132 and 133
Off Broadway
On Broadway
London rehearsals
Smash hit
Rewards

Production photographs reproduced courtesy of Martha Swope (New York City) and Nobby Clark (London). Unless otherwise credited, all other photographs are from Elizabeth Quinn's private collection.

Prologue

I first met Elizabeth Quinn in July 1981 during the first week of rehearsals for the London production of *Children of a Lesser God*. At that stage, I knew nothing of the war games erupting in the tense and emotional sessions in the rehearsal studio. All I found was a group of people locked in studied concentration of the complex work they were embarking on. The cast sat in a circle on functional wooden chairs. Elizabeth was not at the centre of that work session but there was a vibrant alertness and awareness about her which commanded attention. Whatever else she had, this young woman certainly had presence. She also had considerable beauty. The large, brown eyes were watchful, welcoming, with a hint of humour, mischief almost, in their sparkle. She had long dark hair loosely curled onto her shoulders, a wide flashing smile and a trim slender figure dressed that day in jeans, woollen shirt and a casual waistcoat.

I was meeting her for an interview. A year earlier, in New York, in the space of twenty-four hours, I had seen a matinée of *Children of a Lesser God* on Broadway, met Phyllis Frelich (the deaf actress who created the leading female role and on whose experience the play was largely based) with her husband Bob Steinberg at a Sardi's party and then attended the 1980 Tony Awards presentation ceremony at which *Children* received the best play award and Miss Frelich and her co-star John Rubinstein were named as best actress and best actor. The first viewing of the play was a powerful experience. It fulfilled, it seemed to me, most of the requirements of drama. It touched basic nerves of human existence beyond its first attention to the dilemma of deafness. It was informative about an area of life into which we are too rarely taken; it had conflict, progression and characters who developed during our two-and-a-half hours in their company. It also struck a deep emotional chord while working towards a commendably unsentimental conclusion.

The impact of the play was intensified for me when, on leaving the theatre, I found a deaf woman weeping piteously on a seat in the foyer, uttering an eerie wailing noise. I could only imagine that the play had brought home to her the anguish of her own situation.

As Arts Editor of *The Standard* in London, working the rich seam of the performing arts in London, I was determined to alert British theatre audiences to the quality of this play when it arrived, as it surely would, in our own country. I made sure that I would be the first to interview the actress who took the leading role of Sarah Norman. So it was that, a few days after she had made her first trans-Atlantic crossing, I sat for an enjoyable hour with Elizabeth Quinn and her sign-language interpreter in the Mermaid Theatre bar and had the pleasure of introducing her, through *The Standard*, to London theatregoers.

I was intrigued by this profoundly deaf young woman, who remained steadfastly silent yet spoke with dancing hands and animated facial expressions which had an eloquence of their own. I wanted to know more about the life which had brought her to such a commanding and deeply-felt performance on the stage. We met casually and by chance around the Mermaid a couple of times thereafter, and I joined in her celebration after the first night, but I learned little more about her until the night she won the Society of West End Theatre's best actress award. I knew that she would not know many people in the audience of British actors, actresses, writers, producers and directors in the Café Royal that evening, so took care to give her my own congratulations as the dinner broke up. After a few words exchanged through her interpreter, we became separated in the crush but she lingered for a while with my wife, Penny.

As we drove home, Penny complimented Elizabeth's attractive voice. I was astounded. I wondered how much wine she had drunk during the evening. To my knowledge, Elizabeth did not have a voice. But Penny persisted: they had had a perfectly ordinary conversation, with the actress lip-reading. A few days later, my colleague at *The Standard*, Valerie Grove, went off to interview Elizabeth on the strength of her award and to discover how she was leading her life in London. She returned to tell me that the interview had been conducted verbally without the help of an interpreter and proceeded to make that the theme of an excellent article.

Biographies, these days, are too often written when the subject is too young or too 'hyped' to be of lasting interest. This, I hope, is a special case. As I have discovered through many conversations with her, Elizabeth is not just a bright and charming girl who has overcome the disadvantages which life has placed unfairly in her path. She is more complicated than that. She is a mature woman who has grown through experience, an engaging mixture of wisdom and enthusiasms. She has a disarming vulnerability but can also use this as an effective weapon to win over an opponent. If we were at odds during our discussions she would regularly remind me, 'Don't forget, English is only my second language,' American Sign Language coming definitely first. I never did quite find the answer to that. She will welcome and want to learn from what others might consider a most wounding criticism but will take intense personal insult from what she detects to be an unsympathetic facial expression. She can be tough and is a bare-knuckle fighter in argument. Imperfect as we all are, she can occasionally be unforgiving, particularly if she feels she has been condescended to or misrepresented. She is also a thoughtful, caring and unwaveringly loyal friend to those she admits to her wide and international circle of companionship. She is intelligent, endlessly curious and courageous, sometimes to the point of reckless folly.

That courage is reflected in her story. The world of the deaf, as I came to understand, has tensions and politics of its own which the so-called 'hearing world' too little understands. Yet even in that complex silent society, Elizabeth was an exception. She lost her hearing in early childhood but those few years were a sufficient foundation for her to be able to use her voice later, even though she could not hear it herself. She was brought up in a hearing family environment and that family, for all their several misfortunes, raised her with an attentive interest in the things of conventional life from which other deaf youngsters would be excluded.

From that family base, Elizabeth went on to spend long years in deaf institutions and social surroundings where the inhabitants had a deaf culture — held at times with defiant pride — with which she was unfamiliar and into which she remained for a long time uninvited. She was between two worlds and that factor was almost as significant as the lack of hearing itself.

Elizabeth is the product of a rare set of circumstances which have brought her often to the edge of defeat and, less frequently, to soaring elation. From years of insecurity and self-doubt she has found the confidence and self-reliance to lead a full and participating life which has allowed a concern for others to be added to the concentration on mere survival. For all the setbacks she encountered, some inner strength kept her going. Quite what the nature of that strength is lies almost beyond identification; but it has something to do with the capacity of the human spirit to prevail and to aspire, and from that we can all learn and benefit.

Michael Owen
London, 1983

ONE

London 1981

Just after 9.30 p.m. on 25 August 1981, the capacity first-night audience at London's Mermaid Theatre broke into a spontaneous outburst of applause quite different from the usual sort of show-business ovation which can be a predictable part of the theatrical opening-night ritual. It was an involuntary response from the 750 people in the Mermaid's brick-walled auditorium to the highly-charged emotional voyage on which they had been taken for the past two-and-a-half hours. It came as an act of release, of expiation almost, from an audience which had been transfixed and captivated by the events played out on a bare stage furnished only with a couple of benches and a blackboard. The clamorous noise was repeated within minutes as a slender figure in simple red blouse and blue denims stepped to the front of the stage. Alone, in a sea of sound she could not hear, Elizabeth Quinn was experiencing the extraordinary acclaim given by theatre audiences to a sudden 'discovery' and, for her, the rapturous approval extended that night was a significant turning point in her life. Elizabeth had been deaf since the age of two. Now, at thirty-three, she was at last receiving the professional recognition she had sought throughout her adult years. That first night at the Mermaid Theatre was the foundation for a new confidence which would take her to an independence she had hardly dared hope for from three decades of silence.

The play that evening was the London premiere of *Children of a Lesser God* by American author Mark Medoff. It had travelled from its genesis as a workshop production in the drama department of New Mexico State University to its first professional run in Los Angeles, and thence to New York where it had established itself as the Broadway hit of the previous season.

Children of a Lesser God is primarily a love story between a deaf girl student and a speech-therapist tutor at an American college for the deaf. It also follows the girl's struggle to establish her own self-determined independence away from the condescension of the hearing world and the tribal claims of the deaf world. The student, Sarah Norman, is caught between, on the one hand, the demands of fellow students grouping for direct action to win social equality for the deaf and, on the other hand, the seemingly unbridgeable gap of understanding between the deaf and the hearing which jeopardises her relationship with the tutor, James Leeds. The action of the play is conducted by the cast simultaneously in speech and sign language. The leading actress's performance is given solely in sign and, fully within the terms of the drama, is interpreted by the actor playing James Leeds — with the exception, that is, of one harrowing moment when the girl is driven beyond endurance to express herself vocally with an unearthly scream.

The events of the play are inevitably bound up with the life of the leading actress. Medoff had written the piece for the deaf American actress Phyllis Frelich, who originated the role and went on to win Broadway's highest accolade for her performance. Medoff insisted that in future productions the part could only be played by a deaf actress who would bring her own understanding to the character of Sarah. It was to the cathartic nature of the performance, not least, that the London audience had so instinctively responded while at the same time loudly applauding the commanding contribution of the English actor Trevor Eve who played James Leeds. The critics, though in more measured terms, did the same the next day.

The decisive day had not started well for Elizabeth Quinn. She awoke at 5.00 a.m. and was instantly gripped by nausea at the thought of the responsibility ahead of her that evening. She was distanced by 3000 miles from family and friends for the first time in her life and had been in Britain barely a month. She was without professional training and knew that she had just her limited experience in deaf theatre in America, the knowledge gleaned from a spell as understudy in the New York production of the play and her own instinct to get her through one of the most awaited first nights of the year in the acknowledged theatre capital of the world. She was also fully aware that she was facing the single most important event of her life thus far — whichever way it turned out.

Conventional alarm clocks are of no value to the deaf. Elizabeth's alarm was a clock wired to a lamp which flashed at the required time. She also has her own internal body-clock which functions with uncanny accuracy. On the morning of 25 August neither were needed. At dawn, she looked down from her seventh-floor flat in St John's Wood across the roof-tops of London and the warmth of remembering a similar view in the film of *Mary Poppins* was replaced by cold fear. The early awakening was not just an inconvenience. An actor's energy is required at the end of the day, when everyone else is winding down. As well as holding her nerve, she now had to harbour that energy and save it until she stepped on stage some fourteen hours away. She dressed and left the apartment to try to walk off the growing tension. The only company on the early-morning streets were the milkmen, newspaper delivery boys and the first office workers on their way to another routine day. There was a comforting normality about the scene but the very ordinariness of the surroundings offered a false consolation:

It was going over and over in my mind. Would I be good enough? I did not know if I had the power to stay in character right through the play, the strength to open up and give what the character needs. Would Trevor and I really come together and make it work? I had the feeling that Trevor would have enormous acclaim, that people would respond to the play, but what would they say about me and would I be able to deal with it? I wanted to do well. I so badly wanted to make a success of it. As I walked and saw other people going about their daily business I began to feel more fatalistic about it. I thought, OK, well I'll just do the best I can and if I don't make it this time there will always be another chance. I can quite easily withdraw when there is pressure on me. It is a protective thing. But I

knew this time, even while I was thinking like this, that it
was dangerous. I was opting out of the responsibility but
by the end of the day I would have to face it.

Elizabeth returned to her flat and occupied herself with
domestic chores. Her first call was to be at the theatre for a last
rehearsal which started at 2.00 p.m. Against conventional
notions of theatrical glamour, the leading lady set off for her big
first night by Underground, taking the Bakerloo Line south to
the Embankment, and then walked beside the Thames the
remaining half mile to the theatre as she had become accustomed to doing during the previous four weeks of rehearsals.

Those rehearsals had been exceptional by any standards,
accompanied by rows, tears, misunderstandings and tensions
way beyond the theatrical norm. It had not just been a case of
the deaf and hearing worlds colliding uncomfortably together
but had involved differing personalities and styles of work. The
American director, Gordon Davidson, who had supervised the
development of the play and staged its production in Los
Angeles and New York, had made it clear from the outset that
he wanted to re-explore the work with his London cast. Through
the work of his own Mark Taper Forum theatre in Los Angeles,
Davidson had an outstanding reputation in the United States as
an adventurous director and he was not going to take the soft
option of just recreating the New York version. Trevor Eve, a
strong, assertive individual, had arrived at rehearsal with a full-
blooded determination to break through and conquer the most
challenging role of his career. Elizabeth, for her part, was
plunged into a set of working conditions the like of which she
had never known before:

> When they started talking about opening the play up and
> improvizing their way into it, I was terrified. I had no
> training and I had no idea how to go about it. In New York
> I had hidden behind Phyllis Frelich's characterization but
> Gordon was not going to let me do that here. Trevor would
> come at me with an idea and I could not respond. He
> would get impatient and I would just withdraw into

myself. I spent most of two weeks in tears before it began to get better. It was a nightmare.

With the thoughts of those turbulent rehearsals still fresh in her mind, Elizabeth found that the journey to the theatre posed its own threats. She felt the subject of unwarranted attention in the train, as though the harmless strangers were somehow about to pass judgment on her. Trying not to let her nervousness show, she again sank back within herself and wondered what she was doing in London and why she had let herself in for such an ordeal. As she walked alongside the river from the Embankment Station the sight of the rippling water stirred in her waves of homesickness and nostalgia for the simplicity of her childhood at home in West Haven, Connecticut. She recalled the times spent on the West Haven beach where she and her younger brother, Billy, spent carefree days on the sand and in the sea. In her mind's eye she saw again the familiar sight of her mother going to buy ice-cream, a small figure determinedly pushing through the crowd. She remembered her father, who had emerged from fifteen years of alcoholism to become a loving parent whose advice and guidance had given her new courage. The memories were dispelled when she arrived at the complex intersection by Blackfriars Station with its cluster of traffic islands and converging streams of traffic. No one had explained and she had not discovered that there was a pedestrian subway under the junction, so she diced once more with the tangle of cars, taxis and lorries. Across the road there was the encouraging familiarity of the café, where she was already known to the friendly staff, and then a quick raid on the kiosk under the railway bridge for a supply of the chocolate which gave her the same calming satisfaction as a smoker takes from his cigarettes.

After twenty years of colourful existence in a converted riverside warehouse, Lord Bernard Miles's Mermaid Theatre now occupied purpose-built premises on the first three floors of a new office block with the stage door secreted in a quiet cul-de-sac. Once through that door Elizabeth was reunited with the two people she knew best in London. The first was Jean Worth,

an American girl who had been the interpreter on the Broadway production of *Children of a Lesser God.* She had been sent to
London with the play, and the friendship which had developed
between the two women in New York had deepened. (It was
also Jean Worth who had taught Trevor Eve the skills of
American Sign Language.) The second was the director Gordon Davidson. Elizabeth had known him only slightly by the
time they started work together in London and had viewed him
with a degree of mistrust at the outset but the support he had
given her during the difficult weeks of rehearsal had finally
convinced her that he was on her side.

The afternoon rehearsal was a positive session for Elizabeth as
she filled in more detail to her performance, to the approval of
the director. She hoped desperately that she would retain the
same detail for the evening's show. By the time Davidson had
concluded his final notes of advice to the cast, however, it was
almost four hours later. It was nearly 6.00 p.m. when Elizabeth
returned to her dressing room. Telegrams and flowers from
friends and well-wishers were arriving by the minute bringing
their own pressures as a tangible reminder that this, indeed,
was the first night. It was at this point that time seemed to slip
into a new and faster dimension, hurtling her towards the 7.00
p.m. curtain time — although this production, in fact, had no
curtain.

The dressing room offered precious little comfort, with its
linoleum floor and basic shower installed in one corner of the
cramped quarters. The furniture comprised just one clothes
cupboard, a long make-up table and two functional chairs.
With the whiff of fresh paint still in the air, only the dozen light
bulbs ranged beside three small mirrors suggested that the room
was in a theatre at all. Beneath the make-up table there was a
sun lounger on which Elizabeth tried to grab some rest. She had
no sooner lain down than the 'half' was called — the theatrical
convention of warning that curtain time is, not half-an-hour
away as one might guess, but thirty-five minutes. Jean Worth
came in as Elizabeth assembled her costume and make-up and
tried to dilute the tension with casual chatter of hair-styles and

fashion. Elizabeth could not be so easily distracted. She had not had the essential minutes she had promised herself to prepare for the performance. She asked her friend to leave and sat alone, concentrating on thoughts of her mother, her brother and the father who had been her main source of support until his death. All too soon there came the interruption of a light flashing in her room, the signal that it was time to go downstairs to take her place beside the stage for the beginning of the play.

She made her way down the stairs and through the customary clutter of backstage theatre to join the rest of the cast in the wings. Elizabeth and Trevor Eve hugged each other as much for mutual support and wishes of luck as to establish the bond between them on which the play's success must largely depend. Then she stepped to one side into a dark corner only just out of sight of the audience and, in a small space bounded only by a curtain and a bare brick wall, did something she had never done before:

I prayed to my father. 'Be with me. I'm scared. Show me the way, let me open up, let me give.' I felt my family was not there, my friends were not in the audience, the people I had been close to and trusted were not there. I had to do this completely on my own. My father had always been a symbol of security for me, a figure of strength. I could feel him urging me on. I could picture him. I could see his rugged face and silver, wavy hair, his smile and his strong arms and hands. It was like an elbow pushing me on as if he was saying: 'This is no big deal. You go out there and do it.'

She came out of the reverie and just had time to sign 'Good Luck' to Trevor Eve waiting in the opposite wing before a tap on the shoulder from the assistant stage manager told her it was time to take her place on stage. She walked out into the darkness, shaking violently.

Children of a Lesser God opens to a blacked-out stage and to the sound of a solo piano playing the mounting melody line of 'Prayer', from Keith Jarrett's *Death and the Flower*. The lights rise slowly to show the two principal characters on stage at the height of an argument, an argument to be played out fully at the climax of the play. Sarah is squatting on all fours in obvious distress while James stands above her. From the moment Elizabeth took her first position on stage a new force came to her aid:

> I got out there and suddenly I was thinking about all the things that had happened to me. I had the feeling of being on a high. I knew this was make or break. I could feel the music through the stage, I could feel it through my hands. It starts low and then gets heavier. It became higher and higher and I could feel it coming to a crescendo and as it did the energy built up in me. It got stronger and stronger. It seemed to be filling me up. I was ready to go. I had never known that feeling before, nothing as powerful as that. In all my other work and rôles it was as if I had been toying with being an actress. I was ready to be open more than I had ever been in my life before.

That openness was tested immediately. The play's action begins with Sarah's concluding lines of the argument, a despairing assessment of the state of her life which rises to a declaration of defiant independence. The speech is a curiosity in several ways as it is given in sign language only and left uninterpreted — a symbol of that defiant attitude.

American Sign Language is a free form of communication relying more on images and concepts than neat grammatical precision. It can condense a statement into a single gesture with its use of facial expression and body language. In ASL, the opening speech Elizabeth signed before making her first hasty exit from the stage would read: 'ME HAVE NOTHING. ME DEAFY. SPEECH INEPT, INTELLIGENCE — TINY BLOCKHEAD. ENGLISH — BLOW AWAY. LEFT ONE YOU. DEPEND — NO. THINK MYSELF ENOUGH. JOIN, UNJOINED ...'

Author Medoff has offered his own translation of that speech: 'I HAVE NOTHING; NO HEARING, NO SPEECH, NO INTELLI- GENCE, NO LANGUAGE. I HAVE ONLY YOU. I DON'T NEED YOU. I HAVE ME ALONE. JOIN, UNJOINED ...'

If that speech charted the progress of Sarah Norman, Elizabeth was also aware that it was directly relevant to her own life:

> It said so much about what was true to me. To be deaf and not to be able to speak. Because you have no language people always thought you were not intelligent. For so many years I did feel I had nothing. That I was less than other hearing people and could not be useful. There was an image which came to me which I used to think about in rehearsal. It was of me being chained to the floor while others stood around all pointing at me. It meant I could not do anything for myself. I couldn't do anything unless I was told to by teachers or parents or other condescending people and then I would respond accordingly. I used to depend on so many people, too many people, and they were always men — my father, my brother Billy, lovers or directors. The last man I depended on was the director Gordon Davidson. He had helped me and led me into the play. But I knew by coming to London I was going to have to stand on my own and be independent no matter what happened. That was me — unjoined.

Again and again, the words and thoughts of Sarah Norman found an echo in her own existence. First, the anger and frustration of being passed over as a second-class citizen, denied an individuality of her own because her communication was limited. Then, on a gentler level, the innate intelligence, the almost childish sense of fun and the capacity to give love. By drawing on her own experience and bringing to it both her personal and her actress's intuition she was able to bring Sarah vibrantly to life.

Trevor Eve, coming from a different direction with his Royal Academy of Dramatic Art training and his own inquiring mind, also proved his mastery not just of one of the most technically demanding new roles of recent years, with its requirements of synchronised verbal and signed speech (neither exactly fitting the other), but also of the many-faceted character of James Leeds. Leeds, who is never off stage throughout the show, is the controlling pivot of the play. Eve's responsibility was huge. It was also his first major London play after a highly popular television series, 'Shoestring'. He had turned down a season with the Royal Shakespeare Company to take the play and, as *Children of a Lesser God* was already a proven hit on Broadway, the blame for a failure in London would be aimed mainly at him.

Come the interval, Gordon Davidson was able to visit a perspiring Miss Quinn in her dressing room and tell her it was a good first night and he was proud of her. It still took her several deep breaths to get out of the safety of her room and on her way back to the stage for Act II.

The second half opened with Elizabeth already seated on a bench facing the audience as she makes up her face for a bridge party that is about to take place on stage. When the lights came up that night it was the first time she was consciously aware of the audience. During the first half she had felt distanced from the tiered auditorium as though there was a film of gauze between the stage and the rest of the house, as though the action was taking place in an inner box on stage. Now, for the first few rows at least, she could actually see the whites of their eyes.

The audience had relaxed into the play's method of combining signed and spoken speech and was noticeably more responsive, both to the humour of the piece and to the conflict as the deaf and hearing worlds clashed and ricocheted off each other. Chiefly, it was caught up in the relationship between the two protagonists. The performance swept along to its conclusion. Lights down and suddenly Elizabeth was off stage and it was over.

As the cast assembled themselves speedily for their rehearsed order of curtain calls a sense of euphoria was breaking out backstage to the sound of the ovation that was already underway in the auditorium. Elizabeth had no way of knowing of the audience's excitement and she looked anxiously from one face to another. Trevor Eve was grinning broadly and signed: 'They loved it.' Ed Kelly, a hearing-impaired actor from America who had been brought over for the London production, had got the message and was signing animatedly: 'We're a hit.' In quick succession the actors returned to the stage to take their first bows. Then it was Elizabeth's turn.

> When I walked out I did not look up until I had got around the bench and to the front of the stage. They all stood up. I bowed and then I came up. For the first few rows I could see the faces, then further up they were shadows and then just silhouettes. I could see tears in some faces, I could see hands clapping, people clapping above their heads, some were waving programs. Some were signing to me: Terrific (two palms raised). When I came out it had felt unreal, as though I was not there. It was cool, I was floating. Now I could feel the vibration of the noise they were making through my feet. I began to feel dizzy. All I could see in front of me was movement in the audience. It looked like the waves of the ocean. I could not believe these people were responding to me.

Trevor Eve took his bow to another roar of acclaim, the curtain call was repeated and the company joined together on stage to share the applause. Relief and joy mingled in equal quantities backstage as the actors hugged each other in the emotion of the moment. Gordon Davidson sped from his seat in the stalls to register his satisfaction with their achievement. Author Mark Medoff arrived with his own invaluable congratulations and took Elizabeth aside to offer her his personal thanks.

The actors headed for their dressing rooms. Trevor Eve disappeared into his room, to a popping of champagne corks. Elizabeth, with Jean Worth, found the sanctuary of her own room, showered hastily and changed into the one evening dress she possessed, bought only two days previously from a boutique in Covent Garden. The corridors around the dressing rooms filled up with backstage visitors and Press photographers. Elizabeth greeted them in a dazzling white dress which, by now, matched her wide smile. Two deaf women from the audience arrived to present their deeply-felt appreciation of Elizabeth as they feared their triumphant waving of their programmes from the rear of the theatre might have gone unnoticed. But despite the general elation, Elizabeth's satisfaction was tinged with one profound regret. Her family and the friends she had been closest to were not there to witness her success and neither were they there to join in her celebration.

The main centre for the evening's celebration moved from the theatre to the Laguna restaurant in St Martin's Lane in the heart of the West End's theatre-land. The first-night audience had been a high-profile affair with a generous proportion of the leading figures of London theatre and those actors, actresses, directors and producers were the guests at the first-night party.

They were all strangers to Elizabeth and she in turn was decidedly a stranger to this apparently glamorous side of theatrical life. She was unsure of how she should behave and of what she should be saying. It was not because she was deaf but because of her unfamiliarity with the conventions of the occasion and an inhibiting sense of shyness. The party was spread over two floors of the restaurant and, while most of the revellers were bunched upstairs, Elizabeth and Jean Worth went to the quieter room below to join a half-empty table. She was still in a mild state of shock at the events of the evening. Then an unknown man presented her with a poem dedicated to her which he had just written on a restaurant napkin. When he had gone it was explained to her that the man was the poet, Adrian Mitchell. A messenger was sent from the floor above to say that people were looking for her and wanting to meet her. Trevor Eve searched her out with a bottle of champagne and told her she was the best actress he had worked with. The party continued well beyond midnight and in the early hours of the morning Elizabeth and Jean Worth made their farewells and departed into the street in search of a taxi.

It was 2.00 a.m. by the time she was back in the St John's Wood apartment she had left so many hours earlier. Her body felt limp with fatigue but although she was promptly into bed all sleep eluded her. Her mind was exclusively occupied with the sight of the audience in the steeply-raked Mermaid Theatre auditorium as they gave her the ovation she had won so very much by her own efforts. The movement of the hands, faces and bodies reminded her of the sea, a recurring image to which she is

regularly drawn. She had grown up beside the ocean in Connecticut and the sea had been a constant source of comfort and
succour to her.

> The sea has so much power. It has always given me
> confidence, has always been a person to me, somebody out
> there. Whenever I became depressed or indecisive about
> something important, I have always found myself drawn
> to the sea. I can walk on the beach and be quiet, just
> ponder, and when I walk away something good usually
> happens. I understood it when I saw the audience. It was
> the same feeling. It was like the sea. It meant approval. I
> felt: 'Now I can go on.'

TWO

Childhood

Elizabeth Ann Quinn made her entry into the world in St Francis Hospital, Port Jervis, in up-state New York. By her mother's recall, the event was not without at least one or two of the trappings of show business — an interest which was to occupy the Quinn household almost to the point of obsession in the years to come. The year was 1948 and the first baby to be born to the Quinn household was expected to arrive at the end of July. When Anita Quinn's labour started, two weeks early, the only suitcase to hand was an ornate silver case which she used to carry her tap shoes and other accessories to and from her dance classes and with that rather gaudy valise she made herself ready to be taken to hospital. Despite the speed of events which rushed her into St Francis Hospital the labour was a long one but Anita Quinn still retains the clear memory of the sound of a band practising in a field adjoining the hospital grounds. It was later discovered to be The Teen Times Band, a junior ensemble which played its way repeatedly through the same set of show songs. Elizabeth Quinn eventually made her entrance to that unlikely fanfare and in many an Irish home in Port Jervis that night there were celebrations to mark the first arrival of a new generation.

Port Jervis lies some eighty miles north-west of New York City, settled in the Delaware valley and occupying an important junction which made it a natural centre for the railroad in the early part of the century. Employment created by and connected with the railroad was available and the growing town found itself occupied by communities of Irish, Italian, German and British immigrants as well as those who traced their American ancestry back some years further. Amid the

Irish contingent were the families of the Quinns and the Reillys, both of whom were third-generation American Irish and both of whom traced their antecedents back to County Galway where branches of the families still live today.

It came as no surprise, therefore, and no one disapproved, when it became known in the 1920s that two of the youngest members of the two families, Anita Reilly and Jack Quinn, had taken a shine to each other across the classroom at St Mary's Parochial School, at the tender age of seven. The pair grew up together, moving at the same time to Port Jervis High School (where their most formal date was for the graduation party at the age of thirteen) and thereafter accompanying each other to the high-school proms while also moving among a wider circle of friends and meeting less formally at other children's homes. They were also regularly at each other's homes where both sets of parents kept close-knit families. Neither family was in any way particularly well off but nor did they seem to lack for anything.

Jack was a budding athlete with a growing interest in football. He played in the back field with such ability that he was recruited for the Port Jervis High School team, where he distinguished himself with outstanding player awards in inter-college series. Jack was rapidly acquiring the physique to accompany his footballing prowess. His thoughts on a future career were running towards accountancy but when he went to St Bonaventure University in Olean, New York at the age of seventeen, it was the brown and white football shirt with the number 34 on its back that was commanding most attention. Anita visited Jack most weekends at St Bonaventure or Jack would return to Port Jervis to visit the Reillys. It was on such a weekend that the couple were at home in Port Jervis listening to the broadcast of a football game on the radio when the programme was interrupted to announce the United States's entry into the Second World War.

Jack Quinn joined the US Army as First Lieutenant. He was six feet two, weighed 220lbs and with his handsome, open face cut quite a figure in his uniform. He was posted first to Oregon then to North Africa, and saw action in Italy. Anita took up full-time work on the office staff of an automobile business in Port Jervis. They kept up a regular correspondence during Jack's war service with Anita making a daily visit home at lunchtime to see if another letter had arrived and been propped up in the familiar place where her mother always left Jack's latest letters. There were other letters crossing between Europe and America from Jack to both sets of parents. In one of these letters Jack asked his mother to buy an engagement ring for Anita. On his return from the war, Anita vaguely noticed some occasional changes in Jack's personal behaviour but she quickly dismissed them and there was no stinting on the celebrations of the marriage and the happiness of the newly-wed couple. Jack went back to college and they picked up their familiar routine of weekly visits.

On his return to college, it became clear that Jack had a potential for professional football and this was confirmed with the arrival of a certain Mr White, who called at St Bonaventure in the course of his duties of scouting the campus circuit on behalf of the New York Yankees in search of new talent. Jack was invited to step up into the big league and join the Yankees.

The professional game had its drawbacks. Jack settled into the team but the couple found they were being separated more and more. The Yankees had a coaching base at Fairfield, Connecticut, which Anita could sometimes visit but they also played regularly further afield in Kentucky. Of the two, it was Jack who was the more unsettled by the distances and spells apart and he was no longer giving his full commitment and usual concentration to the game. It was Jack who decided to quit after a year with the Yankees. He returned to Port Jervis, the couple moved in with parents and Jack took up a job as an insurance salesman with Anita frequently accompanying him on his rounds. Almost two years to the day after their wedding, it was confirmed that Anita was pregnant. The news was greeted with joy and also with the unspoken assumption from both parents that the infant would be a boy.

Anita's admission into hospital, and the birth of their

daughter, was in the end so sudden that no one had had the time to think of buying baby clothes. Jack was sent off to assemble a hasty wardrobe and came back with the most expensive and extravagant dress he could find. Anita remembers that first dress as the start of a long process by which Jack Quinn lavished everything he could on Elizabeth Ann. The Quinns set up home in a four-room apartment in the same district of Port Jervis where they had always lived and some twenty-two months later the family became four with the arrival of their son, Billy.

Elizabeth proved an energetic and inquisitive child. She quickly learned to walk and showed an early facility with her hands whether they were holding a pencil or a needle. She also began to talk early and very distinctly.

From her first years she always referred to her father by his Christian name but unlike anyone else in the family she called him Jackie:

> I did not call him Jack because I never knew his name was Jack. At least, not until much later. I believe it must have been some hearing fault at that stage. I probably also called him Jackie because I wanted to sound grown up. I always wanted to sound grown up. My mother never liked me calling him Jackie, especially on the bus or in public anywhere. She worried that people might think she was having an affair with someone other than my father.

A pattern had emerged that, while Jack Quinn would be the doting parent, enveloping his daughter with love and concern, the discipline was left to Anita.

The only real blight on the family's fortunes was that Jack Quinn was becoming increasingly discontented with his job as an insurance salesman. He seemed unsuited to the demands of door-to-door selling and collecting money. The disenchantment coincided with the start of a scattering of the wider Quinn family in Port Jervis. His mother moved to Connecticut to help nurse her daughter there and his brother-in-law, who worked on the railroad at Port Jervis, moved to Connecticut to take a similar job at another large rail yard at New Haven. The word came back that there were good jobs to be had with the rail company there. It was decided that the family would move to New Haven and start a new future with Jack employed shunting trains. The move was successfully achieved but it was only a matter of weeks before a new and darker influence entered all their lives when Elizabeth, still only two years old, was struck with a series of illnesses.

Measles, mumps and a virus infection were diagnosed in succession but the Quinns also noticed that an odd syndrome had crept into Elizabeth's speech pattern. She was no longer pronouncing the ends of words with her usual clarity, though she herself appeared unaware of any difficulty. Anita Quinn mentioned this minor defect to the doctor who had treated Elizabeth for the virus infection. Without any outward show of concern he recommended that Elizabeth might be taken to see a specialist. As he wrote out a note for the appointment to be made, Anita noted the few words that were to change their lives. The simple letter of appointment recommended that Elizabeth be examined for a possible hearing loss.

Anita Quinn recalls: 'I was devastated. We all were, though Elizabeth was too young to understand what was going on. We took her to the specialist. The first meeting was just a preliminary interview and we were told to go back again later for tests. I was very upset. I was just a wreck.' The tests concentrated on investigating Elizabeth's response to sound and the results were uniformly depressing. They showed that a nerve in the middle ear was failing. Events took on a remorseless pace of their own and it was apparent to the family that Elizabeth was losing her hearing and losing it fast. Anita Quinn: 'We were in shock. It was a very bad period in our lives. We kept looking for an answer, for a different answer, for someone to say this was not happening. We got very nervous. At that time I do not think Elizabeth fully realised what was happening but it must have been very frightening for her.'

It was the start of a series of rounds to different specialists as the family searched for an answer to Elizabeth's hearing problem, hoping always that the next appointment would bring the consolation that she was suffering just some temporary defect, but coming away in utter dejection with confirmation that the hearing loss was increasing and was probably permanent. The visits fell into a pattern whereby Anita Quinn, Elizabeth and Billy would go together and then bring the latest news home to their father. Jack Quinn was plunged into the deepest despair at the fate which was consuming his precious daughter and it was Anita Quinn who had to shoulder the burden of arranging and carrying out the visits to the various specialists. The family was also running up medical bills which it could ill afford, but financial considerations were a low priority and somehow they kept finding the money for one more appointment, one more opportunity to be told that their darkest fears were unwarranted and that a cure could be achieved. That comfort, however, was never available. Elizabeth was just five:

> I remember many visits to doctors. Mother, Billy and I would go together. There was a lot of waiting in hallways, different clinics and different places. We seemed to spend so much time sitting in so many waiting rooms. I would be put in a special room. It was panelled in boards with a lot of holes in them. Like a recording studio, I guess. The rooms were always the same and always with one window in them. Then I would be told to raise my hand if I heard a sound. Mother and Billy were always on the outside and I was alone inside. I could never understand why Billy was not with me. We used to do everything together.

Elizabeth's descent into deafness was not the only change of circumstance affecting the family. The Quinns decided to move home from New Haven a couple of miles down the road to the once favoured resort of West Haven and there they settled in a small but neat two-storey house with just two bedrooms and three downstairs rooms and its own porch and shingle front. The house carried the address of 107½ California Street: it was set back from the road and approached down a narow path leading to their own garden gate and confined patch of land dominated by one large maple tree. The sea front with its enticing beach was just one block and two minutes' walk away. The Quinns were to live in that house for the next twelve years and, though it is looked back on with fondness now, it was also to be the scene of the several crises that beset the family.

Jack Quinn was beginning to drink more regularly and more steadily. It was mainly a flow of beer at that stage and the cause of only mild concern at the time. The violent tensions were to come later. But between the new house and the beach was a sea-front bar called Papa Conti's which was to become known within the family as 'Dad's Hotel'.

Part of the process of settling into the new West Haven community was to enrol Elizabeth at her first school. She joined the kindergarten class of the local parish school, established in recently completed buildings with an adjoining school field, complete with the usual assortment of children's outdoor amusements including a set of swings. The swings provided a consolation all their own to the young child; here she could enjoy an experience unrelated to the problems of communication which she was just beginning to sense. Elizabeth was identified as a bright child and on her first graduation she was promoted to the first grade, but with the added remark that she had a tendency to be withdrawn. Anita Quinn told the school that her daughter suffered from a degree of hearing loss and the suggestion was made that perhaps she should wear a hearing aid. It was the first time that such a device had been mentioned. The teacher had observed also that, as Elizabeth's hearing diminished, she was talking less and her speech was increasingly affected. Anita started taking Elizabeth to a special speech class but the results were not encouraging. 'It got to the stage where I did not want the teacher to tell me what was happening,' she said later.

As Elizabeth's hearing faded a select few sounds embedded themselves in her memory to remain there for the rest of her life. One was of a lullaby her father sang to her: 'Go to sleep for Mommy, go to sleep for Dad . . .' Another was the voice of her brother Billy, aged three. Whenever Billy spoke to her in later life she still heard in her mind's ear the piping young voice.

Billy Quinn, although only three at the time, can remember the onset of Elizabeth's deafness: 'I remember I had to start to talk slower to her than for others so that she could understand. I vaguely remember going round the many specialists, the effort of trying to see if she could function in a hearing environment. There came the realisation that she had some kind of handicap. But I seem to think that Liz was already lip-reading from just as early as I can remember.' Without knowing it, the young child was probably already compensating for her loss of hearing, instinctively:

> I do not think I was aware of what was happening to me at that time. Even at kindergarten I did not realise that I was different. But I do remember a feeling of fear; that I was frightened. I think perhaps I knew there was something so terrifying happening that I blocked it out. But I do remember some sounds. My father's voice was beautiful. I could hear it through my ear and also by vibration. Years later people said he had a great speaking quality. There were other sounds. Billy's voice has stayed with me. And there was an aeroplane I heard. I remember an aeroplane.

Anita Quinn was still seeking different medical advice in the hope that a cure, or at least some optimistic alternative, could be found. She found a new doctor who was the first to suggest that they should approach the American School for the Deaf at West Hartford, Connecticut. Anita fixed an appointment with the president of the school and set off for the meeting in the belief that he might provide another source of advice on what they should do next. 'We had been through so much that it just seemed like another good thing to do just to see what he would say.'

Out of the blue the president proposed that Elizabeth should be enrolled as a resident student of the American School for the Deaf. The spectre that Elizabeth faced some form of institutionalised future had been raised and could not have been more unexpected. Anita Quinn says: 'That was a very bad day. All along we were looking for all the help we could get and we thought we could keep Elizabeth at home. Once we knew she was going to have to stay at that school we had to face it that she was not going to have a normal life.' The prospect of Elizabeth being removed from the family home also cut Billy Quinn deeply: 'That was the first time I knew for sure that there was a difference between Liz and the rest of us. I knew she had to go away for school and for me as a young kid that made me very lonesome.'

The most important decision the Quinns had been required to face was now upon them. Should Elizabeth be sent away at the age of six to a specialised school? Jack Quinn was reluctant to let his daughter be separated from the family:

> My father did not want to accept it. He kept trying to prove that everything was all right because he wanted so desperately to believe it. We had company one day and I remember particularly that my father said to everyone, 'Watch. Watch this.' And he told me to turn around and then he spoke to me and when he had finished speaking I turned to him and smiled and he said, 'See, Elizabeth can hear.' I had not heard anything at all. I never did hear anything but I always turned at the right time. I was learning to be a survivor, you see. I knew right from an early age that I was a problem and I didn't want to be. I wanted my parents' approval. I wanted to be accepted. Billy was the brilliant one, and I wanted to be up there with him.

And so the decision fell largely to Anita Quinn. She was already struggling to find the correct course of action amid the confusion which Elizabeth's hearing problems had brought to the household but she also had the evidence of her own eyes to dictate that some form of assistance or guidance was needed. By this time, if she called to her daughter and the small child's back happened to be turned to her, she knew there would be no response. Anita settled in favour of Elizabeth going to the American School for the Deaf, knowing the pain that would be inflicted on all sides of the family.

She recalls: 'I went along with the idea of the American

School for the Deaf. I thought it would equip Elizabeth for something in life but I didn't realise then we were starting something that was going to go all the way through college for her. But I thought it was for her benefit. There were so many tough decisions to make. I guess sometimes I did the wrong things but if I did, I did them for what seemed to me to be the right reasons at the time. I could not explain it all to Elizabeth. She was too young and I was too upset. There was always doubt. You were never sure if you were doing the right thing. It was heart-breaking.'

The decision was made. Elizabeth was to attend the American School for the Deaf by week and return home each weekend and at the holidays. The only one who was unaware of what her immediate future held for her was Elizabeth and she was to make that discovery very shortly in a day of turmoil and trauma.

THREE

Schooldays

Elizabeth's entry into the American School for the Deaf was delayed by a hurricane which swept west Connecticut and made travelling impossible. The family set off a day late to drive the forty miles up the Merritt Parkway to West Hartford. On arrival they were confronted by a vast and imposing building approached by a tree-lined drive amid parkland. An ornate dome topped by a weather vane commanded the roof while, below, wide steps led between formal columns classically spaced across the frontage past the statue and sculptures of Thomas Gallaudet, the founder of education for the deaf in America and creator of the first sign language. Jack and Anita Quinn with Elizabeth decked out in her best blue dress made their way into this intimidating edifice man-handling one large suitcase between them. They were greeted by a large hall with two grand staircases off it; large portraits hung on the walls and an aquarium of exotic fish was installed on one side. As they went in search of the superintendent's office, it seemed to the Quinns that they had stepped into a set from *Gone with the Wind*. Elizabeth still did not know why they were there:

> I was very scared because we did not live in anything like this sort of place. We lived in California Street in a beach house and this place felt very elegant. There were busts of famous people everywhere with lights on them and it seemed more like a museum. I still had no idea I was going to stay there.

They were greeted by the superintendent who suggested that Elizabeth should change out of her smart dress into play clothes so that she could go and mix with the other children. Elizabeth

24

was taken past classrooms and offices and upstairs to a dormitory where she found that her suitcase had already been placed
on one of the seven beds. When she opened the case she
discovered all her clothes packed inside it, each item bearing a
brand-new name tag.

Jack and Anita Quinn were given an introductory talk by the
superintendent and as they left his office they caught sight of
Elizabeth, through a window, surrounded by a group of girls
who were gesticulating at her, with one larger black girl being
particularly demonstrative. They thought the other girls were
breaking into a fight with Elizabeth. At the sight of his daughter
so alone, so vulnerable and apparently so threatened, Jack
Quinn broke down and rushed to his daughter's rescue
vowing aloud that he would not leave her there. He had to be
restrained by Anita. In that highly charged emotional atmosphere the parents had to make their farewells to Elizabeth:

> I was left in a room, I remember, with a big black girl
> there and some other girls. The black girl was awfully
> wild, throwing her arms around and all the girls were
> signing to me but I did not know what they were saying.
> They were probably saying 'Are you new?' and 'Are you
> deaf?', but I could not understand them. I got scared and I
> cried. My mother and father came but finally they told me
> they had to go and said goodbye. My father was upset and
> wanted to take me home. He would have done if he had
> been on his own but my mother said No and pulled him
> away. For the first time in my life, my father walked away
> from me. I could not understand it. He was crying too.
> This big, powerful man, so strong and so agile, was being
> led away in tears by my mother who looked so small and
> frail. I was very confused and crying myself all the time. I
> think that was the moment when I first thought that I
> really didn't like my mother.

Elizabeth was left among her new schoolmates with whom she
had no means of communication. The head teacher came to her
and insisted she stop crying but all Elizabeth could see was an
extremely animated face mouthing at her and the wagging of an

admonishing finger. The message of what was required of her
failed to penetrate so she continued to cry. She was shut in the
dormitory bathroom until the tears ceased, but even that failed
to work:

> That bathroom was a long narrow room with a long
> bath, a wash basin and a window that had bars on it. It was
> very claustrophobic. There was a mirror but it was too
> high for me to look into. I wanted to look in it, I wanted to
> see something. Maybe I wanted to see myself but I could
> not. I just kept crying and crying and banging on the door.
> I did not understand that I had been put in there to stop
> crying. I would have stopped if I had known that but I had
> no idea what was going on. Finally I got so tired I went to
> sleep on the floor.

Elizabeth was eventually released and put to bed where she fell
asleep exhausted, noticing only that the girl in the next bed
was strapped in to prevent her roaming during the night. It was
hardly a comforting sight. The girl, named Jan, a blonde,
freckled child with a gentle disposition became one of Elizabeth's closest friends during her thirteen years at the American
High School for the Deaf.

Anita Quinn remembers the anguish of that separation to this
day. 'It was extremely hard. I made the mistake of saying to
Jack that he should go and get her when we saw Elizabeth
surrounded by the other girls. That started him saying he was
not going to leave the place without her. We did not go home
that night. Jack's sister-in-law, Ruth Quinn, had invited us to
go to stay at her house so we would not have to be at home
without Elizabeth.'

Elizabeth began her career at her new school with a series of
radical and wholesale adjustments necessary if she was to
adapt to her new life (on her very first morning she had to
remain in the dormitory until the other girls had left, to try to
disguise the fact that she had fouled her bed during the night).
Away from the warm and relaxed atmosphere of her home she
had to come to terms with the fact that she was isolated from her

parents and brother Billy and for the first time had to survive in a deaf and hard-of-hearing community. She would have to accept the discipline imposed by the staff, the regimentation of institutional life, the loss of individuality in community living, the problems of communication by methods with which she was not familiar and, perhaps worst of all, the adjustment to a style of education which was totally foreign to her:

> In the beginning I just could not respond. I was so shocked by what had happened to me. My parents had not sat down and explained to me that they were doing this because they thought it was the best thing. In those days, if you had a deaf child you did not know really what to do. I did not know why I was there. I had been doing so well at kindergarten and there did not seem any reason to change from that. I was very drawn in for those early months.

Elizabeth found herself in a class of ten under the tutorship of Mrs Dunn, a decent woman but one who seemed to a newly arrived child of six to be very strict — an impression reinforced by the formality of pupil-teacher deportment, as can still be seen in the classroom photographs. The emphasis at the school was on raising pupils' hearing thresholds where possible by means of hearing aids and amplification, and on developing speech. With the bulky pack of a Zenith hearing aid strapped to her chest, and uncomfortable earphones clamped on her head, Elizabeth could capture the last vestiges of hearing. Speech lessons were given a priority of one hour every day and the children were encouraged to communicate in speech and also taught lip-reading:

> We were told to use our voices but we felt very funny going round talking to each other when we could not hear each other. We all knew it was senseless but we did what we were told just to prove to the teachers that we were good. We were the best class and we even made fun of the other kids who could not speak as well as we could. It was no real problem for me as I was always speaking at home to Billy and my parents.

While the concentration on speech may have seemed irrational
to the youngsters, who could hear neither themselves nor each
other without the aid of earphones, it had the effect of arresting
the voice deterioration which Anita Quinn had first noticed as
an early symptom of her daughter's hearing loss. It was not until
some years later that Elizabeth began to be self-conscious and
inhibited from using her voice in front of strangers.

There was, however, one regular ordeal which produced
acute anxiety. The teacher addressed the class mainly through a
microphone set up on a stand at the front of the classroom: to
their extreme discomfort, the children would be exhorted to do
the same in turn to the rest of the class. There was no instruction
in the more formal alphabetical sign language of the deaf and
the altogether freer American Sign Language was regarded as a
base gutter language to be rewarded with a punishment if found
in use.

In the safety of the dormitory and anywhere else where they
were unseen the children communicated freely by means of
ASL. At mealtimes in the cafeteria they were forbidden to use
sign language, but they communicated with one another by
subtle facial expressions.

An early incident in Mrs Dunn's classroom gave Elizabeth an
effective pointer to the way she should conduct herself:

> Mrs Dunn was quite hard on a few people and there was
> one girl called Judy who really got it. Mrs Dunn would
> make Judy say a sentence into the microphone but Judy
> just could not do it. Mrs Dunn would really get after her,
> tell her what she was doing wrong and make her do it
> again. Judy would be crying but Mrs Dunn would not let
> her sit down. I think that experience made me determined
> to be a good lip-reader so that I could understand what
> was going on, and to work hard on my speech. I decided
> very early on that I was going to be a survivor.

Meanwhile, Elizabeth began to learn the precious sign language from her friends and was rewarded with a personal name
in sign. It was the sign of two Es on the forehead, given as a

recognition of her intelligence. This acknowledgment was made by her fellow pupils well in advance of the teaching staff, who mistook Elizabeth's early fearful and nervous defences for a lack of ability.

There were still the new disciplines and restrictions to be overcome and that process took considerable time. The experience of being enclosed within a building rather than being allowed to wander West Haven with her brother came as an uncomfortable novelty. The decor was mainly in murky yellows, greys and greens and the ubiquitous fluorescent strip lighting — especially the overhead light which flashed on and off in the dormitory as a morning alarm — became so oppressive that, to this day, Elizabeth will not tolerate such lighting in a room of her own. Lessons, meals and even lavatories were negotiated only with formal queuing and queuing in order of height. An orderly line of children standing to attention was required and if anyone was seen to slouch he or she was likely to receive a slap rather than a verbal reprimand. The structured menus and small portions at mealtimes were also in contrast to life at home. Breakfast was invariably a lumpen oatmeal porridge and the session frequently protracted as staff waited for every child to clear his dish of the hated mixture:

> Coming from a warm and loving family, it was hard. I had been so free, spiritually and physically free. I had been allowed to run and roam as far as I wanted. From that I had come into a completely conformist world and it was a total shock. The food was awful and so different from home where food was important to us, where my mother made great meals and my father made wonderful breakfasts. Every time I put some of that porridge in my mouth I would heave.

There were also pleasures to be discovered and chief among these was the playground with its assembly of equipment including slides, a climbing frame, a see-saw and, most valuable, a particularly high swing which Elizabeth used with such enthusiasm that the playground supervisors stationed themselves at its side as a safety precaution whenever she climbed aboard:

> I was so small that the chains pinched my hands. I used to swing up as high as I could and get level with the top of the swing. Then I would drop down from there just hanging on to the chains with my hands and not using my legs or bottom at all. I loved that playground because I could be free there. Up on the swing I felt closer to God and closer to my family. There was a football field behind the playground and across it I could see right to the horizon. I could see the sun.

There was another ritual to be learned and that was the composition of a regular letter home to parents. Mrs Dunn would supervise their creation and, as Elizabeth recalls, each letter tended to run on the same theme of, 'I am having a good time and Mrs Dunn is very nice.' Any variation on this text tended to be dismissed as unnecessary and summarily rejected. It quickly became practice to write as directed and then look forward to the weekend.

The weekend. That was the time to be cherished. Laundry was packed to be taken home and then there was the blissful reunion with parents and the journey back to West Haven for forty-eight hours of festivity to make up for the separation during the week. Gifts would be waiting at home, sweets and candy, special meals would be cooked and picnics and outings to the beach or the cinema organised. Elizabeth was indulged to the utmost, particularly by her father. The one indulgence that was never granted was the truth — that on Sunday the weekend would end and it would be necessary to return to school. This led to scenes of such dire distress that the family is marked by them today and Billy still carries a loathing for Sunday twenty-five years later. It would start with Jack Quinn's reluctance to begin the journey back to West Hartford; he made it obvious that he would rather have Elizabeth stay home. Anita Quinn would have to counteract her husband's weakness. She knew that Elizabeth had to be taken back to school and somehow the deed had to be done. It was customarily started with a deceit to Elizabeth that they were going for a drive or to visit relatives, but it always ended in West Hartford amidst angry tears.

After a few Sundays Elizabeth began to be familiar with certain landmarks along the route. The one she knew best was a large white, colonial-style building which stood at the turn-off from the North Maine turnpike and was used as a furniture store. That building became a signal to her that she was being returned to school and when it came in sight she broke into hysteria.

Billy Quinn: 'Sunday was always a sad day because Elizabeth was leaving. There were scenes when my father, my mother and Liz would all be crying. I felt sad and confused and felt I was losing my friend. We would drive on the turnpike until we saw this furniture store and then all hell would break out. Liz would be pleading, screaming and shouting "Let's go back!" It was always such an emotional journey and this went on for months.'

My parents had always encouraged me in everything and included me in everything. The one thing they did not tell me was why I had to go away to school. They were so heart-broken they could not bring themselves to do it. I went home every Friday and then when I had to go back to school they were lying to me all the time. We would all get in the car and they would say we were just going for a drive. But every time I saw that furniture store I knew they were taking me back to school and I would scream and scream in the car because I did not want to go back. Still no one explained to me why I had to go away or what it was all about or why they thought it was good for me. Billy was allowed to stay at home. Billy and I did everything together. I could not understand why he was not coming with me. It began in me a feeling of being unloved and unwanted.

Sundays remained a day to be dreaded in the Quinn household, but Elizabeth was very gradually beginning to lose her fear of her new surroundings and once the school routine was in force

again on Monday mornings she began to find her feet among
her new companions. There were even signs of mischievousness
creeping into her conduct. It tended to manifest itself in the
dormitory after lights-out, with surreptitious games that would
result in a spanking with a wooden bat or ruler from a member
of the staff. If the offence was sufficiently grave she would be
taken downstairs to stand in a corner and face the wall in a
position where she could be seen by the staff who were taking
their coffee. If she turned her head a reproving flashlight would
be shone on her. To stand at length in a dark corner was
disorientating for a deaf child, sometimes to the point of nausea.

Growing familiarity put her more at ease in her lessons. She
could feel songs when they were played through the earphones
and from them began to develop a sense of vibrations. In
speech classes, rather than be caught out by a teacher, she tried
to stay ahead and kept herself alert. In academic subjects she
was sometimes found to be day-dreaming: 'The teachers were
always saying, "Pay attention, Elizabeth!"' The truth was that
she was achieving the work required of her and was thereafter
bored. Although she could not hear it, she had a good speaking
voice, but she only used it in class when she was forced to. At
home she talked freely with what Billy described as almost an
aristocratic accent. She also had plenty of volume and on
occasion had to be told to pipe down.

Since sign language was her only way of talking to her fellow
pupils, Elizabeth picked it up rapidly and soon demonstrated it
at home. On one of her early weekend returns home she and
Billy were taken to church by Anita. As the prayers began, she
gestured to them to kneel. Elizabeth hesitated, knowing she
was not supposed to speak in church, then signed to her mother
'It's dirty.' This was the first time her mother saw her use sign
language.

Billy, however, showed a lively curiosity in this strange
business of talking with your hands and was an eager pupil for
Elizabeth's sign lessons:

The other children taught me to sign and when I went

home I taught Billy. Billy picked up all the signs and he would explain to me about hearing people and what they were doing with their voices and their faces. You see, hearing people learn to behave in a certain way and to express their personality through the way they use their voices and their faces. Billy would tell me not just what they were saying, but what they really meant to say, and I would say, 'Oh, I see. That's why her face is like that.' And he'd say, 'Yes, that's right.' It was the same when we were watching television. Billy would interpret the films on television for me. First he would interpret the dialogue verbatim as the actors spoke, then he would quickly explain all the undercurrents of the plot and then go right back into the dialogue. When I was away from home I would go over and over in my head all the things Billy and I had watched together and keep it fresh in my mind so that when I next saw him we could talk about it again. If it was a scarey film, Billy would describe the music to me and the atmosphere and I could feel my hair standing up on end even before anything happened on the screen because Billy let me know exactly how it felt. All of this meant so much to me.

Later, when Billy visited his sister at the American School for the Deaf and met her friends there, he became thoroughly proficient in signing, using all the facial and body mannerisms that are part of the language:

American Sign Language is a much more fluid and expressive form of signing than English Sign Language. Billy eventually got very good at it. He was much, much better than any Certified Interpreter I have ever known, even when he was very young. Just to give an example: there was a bar near our house which was patronized mainly by black people, and they had a black jazz band there. Billy used to stop there on our way to the beach every day and he would interpret the rhythm for me. He knew all the names of the musicians and all the songs and he pulled me into that world. I loved it. It was a new form of communication and it caught my imagination. Later on at school we were taught about rhythm and most deaf children just did not understand it, but I was good at it and that was entirely due to Billy. He taught me. He used his face, his body, anything I could catch on to, to get it across.

Jack Quinn, too, developed a skill a signing and he would interpret television programmes for her in the same way Billy did:

> They both of them had the art of making the actor's voice become visual for me. I honestly feel that is where I got my training for acting. I was fortunate in having two people who were story-tellers, singers and actors in my family. My father was a wonderful story-teller. He would sit me on his knee and tell me stories and even if they were just stories about his friends on the railroad, he would make it so real and so vivid it was like watching a movie. Afterwards I would go over it all in my head and remember my father's face when he was telling the story and the way his eyes smiled and the funny words he used.

By contrast, Anita Quinn, partly from her own conviction and partly acting on the advice from the school, never did enter into sign language. She said: 'I always thought that as she had a voice she should be encouraged to use it so I continued to go on speaking to her. I thought that in the future if she went anywhere just signing and not talking then people would not be able to understand her. I thought from the beginning that even if she refused me I would still talk to her and she could lip-read me. It was not easy and at times it was hard. She thought I should be signing. If I had done so it would have meant everyone in the house was signing with her and I wanted to keep something else there as well. It was done out of love for her but she could not see that at the time, of course. Maybe it did lead to a gap between us.'

The seeds of future conflict were being sown during those early years at school, not least in a cooling of relations between mother and daughter (at least from Elizabeth's side) which would be resolved only much later. Cosseted by her father, the young child felt that her mother was occupying herself elsewhere. The truth was probably as simple as the example forwarded by Anita. While her father was providing the extended welcome on weekends home, Anita was getting on with such basic necessities as taking care of her daughter's laundry. Anita also had to take the onus of financial responsibility for the family. When Jack Quinn came to have long periods out of work, she had to turn out to find work to support the family. Jack Quinn had all the time in the world to take his daughter on his knee and spin those stories:

> My mother did not learn to sign. I would ask her why she did not sign and she always said 'I will learn' but she never did. She was terribly nervous about everything. Her movements were very quick and nervous and she made me nervous. She chain-smoked all the time and she talked so fast that I could not understand her. Every time I would turn to Billy or my father and ask what she had said. When I did ask her to repeat something she would sigh and look exasperated and I could see she was thinking: 'Why didn't you get it first time?'
>
> When she was with her own friends or her relations and laughing with them she was wonderful. But I resented that because she did not share it with me. When I was small I did not like her too much. I think she frightened me and because of that I built up a wall against her. I felt that everything that was wrong was her fault. I did not understand her.

Another source of discord was the divided life Elizabeth was living, sharing herself between school and family. At school she was firmly a member of the deaf world, on equal terms with her peers. At home she was among the hearing world and, although she was not part of it on equal terms with the others, she was learning how to function in that world. There was a further complication that both worlds were highly protected environments for her. The school was an exclusively deaf community cut off from the rest of society, while the anxious care and concern from her family sheltered her from the outside world. All these confusions were surfacing as she was adjusting to the life at the American School for the Deaf and it took fully a year

before she could be counted as a contented pupil. Anita found a
note that Elizabeth had left behind after one visit home. It read:
'I love my school and thank you for sending me there.' That
note meant a great deal to her mother: 'It was the first time I
knew I had done the right thing in sending her there.'

As her school career advanced into its second year, Elizabeth
moved into the first grade and also into a new, larger dormitory
— thirty beds lined neatly along the walls and, down the centre
of the room, a row of yellow tin lockers in which all clothes were
to be stored. It had the look of an army barracks room and the
uniformity did not appeal to her. Her new teacher, for both the
first and second grades, was a Mrs Dedrick, who became a
favourite with Elizabeth, not least because she regularly used
recordings of children's songs and nursery rhymes in her speech
classes. When Mrs Dedrick held a contest to see who could best
memorise a set of ten nursery rhymes, Elizabeth was the winner
and was duly awarded the prize — a harmonica:

> I am deaf. What could I do with a harmonica? But at the
> time I was delighted with it. I did not know any better.

In spite of these high-points, discipline was still a major
problem:

> All the teachers at school were hearing. I remember one
> time when we had been signing to one another in class,
> which was strictly forbidden, and the teacher got up and
> switched off the light. In that way, with a flick of the
> switch, she stripped us of our natural language. We were
> left in the dark, wordless, isolated. But I do not remember
> feeling angry, only guilty because we had upset her.

It was during her second year that Elizabeth made a discovery
which was to cause her much concern. Mrs Dedrick continued
the system of calling children up to the front of the class to speak
through the microphone but almost invariably chose the hard-
of-hearing children rather than the deaf children, as they were
more proficient in speech. A possible reason for this selection

was passed on to Elizabeth by Billy. There was a panel on the wall of the classroom which appeared to be a blackboard, rarely used. Billy had overhead that there was a room behind this panel into which parents were taken. Through the panel they could watch the class at work:

> I thought that was horrible. To have people watching us as though we were animals or something. I hated that.

Like any group of people thrown together at random, the students evolved their own social strata and these were determined by the degree of hearing or deafness in each individual. The pupils with profound hearing loss banded together against the hard-of-hearing and regarded them as second-class citizens. In a group they became confident and even aggressive, using their own propaganda against 'the hearies'. Any deaf child found to have a hard-of-hearing friend was running the risk of being instantly put down by his own deaf group. This burgeoning confidence led to greater rebellion. Lights-out was called at 8.30 p.m., but Elizabeth was used to being allowed up until nearly midnight at home and she initiated robust games in the darkened dormitory.

School work progressed and expanded. She won prizes for handwriting; her art work was taken home proudly for inspection (young Billy was especially impressed with her ability and sensed early on that art was to play an important part in her future). Elizabeth's favoured events were the nature rambles, expeditions into neighbouring woods in search of the local flora and fauna. It was a rare opportunity to get outside school and out of doors was where she preferred to be. Teachers ranged from an elderly lady who did not make too many demands on her pupils to a fiercer virago, who kept a bottle of whiskey in her cupboard and insisted that her charges learn as many national anthems of the world as she could cram into their heads, for no reason that was apparent to anyone other than herself.

There was even a first fluttering brush with the opposite sex when a new boy called Francis arrived from Massachusetts.

Although he was several years older, he was placed in Elizabeth's class, where his obvious maturity won him many admirers:

> He was not very bright for his age, which was why he was put in our class, but we did not realise that. Every time he went by me he used to put his hands on my shoulders and I would feel so beautiful and wanted. And there I was, a very skinny thing in my pony tail and bobby sox.

School had become by now comfortable and familiar but it was still a case of living for the weekends and holidays — those long vacations when she and Billy would run free and West Haven would seem like some enchanted paradise.

West Haven had seen its heyday come and go as an elegant resort town, but with its beach and two-mile strip of fairground amusements hard against the shore it had more than sufficient to please two youngsters on the loose and at that time still attracted trippers and holiday-makers from New York and New England. The town had a gentle and leisurely colonial atmosphere and the amusements area was still holding decay at arm's length, which made it a better bet than Coney Island.

West Haven sits snugly in the curve of Long Island Sound, with two breakwaters approaching each other a mile out to sea to tame the Atlantic rollers. The water is clear and the swimming good. The fairground has been demolished now; but when Elizabeth and Billy were young it was a hustling, raucous, non-stop show with its carousels, the Wild Mouse big dipper, shooting galleries, side-shows, clam bars and 25-cents hot-dog stalls. It was full of noise, from the ringing laughter of the mechanical clown in the Laff-in-the-Dark booth to the equally loud marionette figure of the Laughin' Lady. And there was also mystery, such as the enigmatic figure of Indian Joe who wandered unspeaking through the crowds with his long black hair and feather stuck in his wide-brim hat. These and other characters remain for posterity caught in the murals of Jimmie's restaurant, a thriving eatery which stands where the original Jimmie ran his hot-dog stall and became a celebrity in his own

right for inventing a fast-food delicacy called a charcoal, split
grilled hot dog.

The Quinns lived just a few hundred yards from this gaudy
strip and they could make a few cents stretch out into an
evening's or a whole day's entertainment:

> We had wonderful times there. There was a huge Ferris
> Wheel and when you went over the top you could see
> across the sea for miles. The carousel had beautiful carved,
> painted horses which would go up and down. They had
> gold rings on poles above you as you went round and the
> trick was to time it so you could catch the ring. Billy and I
> became expert at it. In the middle of the carousel there was
> an organ covered in mirror-panel patterns. I could not
> hear it but I could feel the vibration of it. Even waiting to
> go on, seeing the people waiting for something to happen
> was a thrill for us. Then when we were tired we would go
> home with our prizes.

The other delight was the beach, just two minutes' walk from
their home. They were both expert swimmers and were
allowed the run of the waterfront. At other times it would be a
family picnic or Elizabeth would just walk on her own along the
shore. Every summer both kids would be tanned a deep and
healthy brown. Anita Quinn: 'We just lived for those holidays
when the family could be together and we could go to the beach
and have a carefree time. Those days were like a bit of heaven.'

Billy Quinn: 'The beach was the place Liz liked to be and I
am sure it was there she first dreamed of what she might
become, especially later on. We would be there from sun-up to
sun-down. Mom would come with us and that is where a lot of
sense was spoken. It was a great time of sharing, away from the
stress at home. Somehow everything was much freer on the
beach. There were no hang-ups or restrictions. There was
always a crowd there in the summer and we would get friendly
with some of the boys. Deafness was never a problem for Liz
there.'

The days on the beach were the best times of my life. We

became part of it; everyone knew us. We could tell the time by the tide or we would put a stick in the sand and know the time from its shadow. We'd climb over the lifeguard's chair, swim all day long and we even made pets out of the horseshoe crabs. Then Mom would go off to get us an ice-cream from the stand or a soda or a hot-dog from Jimmie's. The sea was my element and I am still drawn to it now wherever I am.

Those were the best of times but away from the beach another dark cloud was gathering over the Quinn family. Jack Quinn was drinking heavily, to the point that he was now a confirmed alcoholic.

FOUR

Family Life

The precise reasons why Jack Quinn took to drink in the alarming manner he did and with such disastrous consequences can only be guessed at. Anita Quinn, seeking to protect her husband's reputation, would rather draw a veil over this period of his life which was spent in weeks at a time of total immersion in alcohol followed by longer periods of abstinence and a return to normality. This was the pattern of Jack Quinn's life for fifteen years or more, with the drinking giving rise to moods of great rage and sometimes violent anger, but alternating with months of rehabilitation when the family would have a caring and apologetic father returned to them. Elizabeth saw the evidence of her father's drinking during her early years at the American School for the Deaf but without understanding its significance. Her absence at school during the week limited her exposure to what was going on; her father tried desperately to make a special effort whenever she was at home and her mother and brother were determined to shield her from the suffering.

Jack Quinn was rescued finally when Alcoholics Anonymous came to his aid and for the last seven or eight years of his life he was once again the devoted parent who earned as well as received the love of his family. But while he was drinking he almost tore the family apart — giving Anita Quinn another set of almost unendurable problems, bringing Billy to a personal conflict of his own, unwittingly causing Elizabeth further confusion through acts of unkindness which he would not soberly have committed and so damaging the family's economic stability they were forced to move through a succession of homes.

All those years ago, when Anita Quinn noticed those subtle personality differences and small changes in behaviour patterns in Jack on his return from war service, an alteration in his drinking habits was a part of them. Like any other young man he had enjoyed social drinking and, as Anita expresses it, had had fun with drink; but on his return from Europe there was a difference. It was not so great that she gave it much concern. She was wise enough to know that many young soldiers who went to the war came back not untouched by their experiences; Jack had told her some of the incidents he had witnessed, including seeing a soldier next to him shot dead in the head during action in Italy. When her father recounted stories of his footballing career, Elizabeth remembers, drink would be mentioned on occasion but in any sporting company of fit young men it would have been more unusual for it to be absent. The early end to Jack's football ambitions might have been a factor, but there was no sign of a direct connection. The crisis of Elizabeth's deafness might well have made its contribution and there were times later when, unfairly, Elizabeth thought she was the sole cause of her father's decline into drink.

The greater influence may well have been simpler: an uncle of Jack's, who was a dashing and romantic figure but also a hopeless alcoholic. Jack Quinn was in thrall to this colourful character and it is possible that he took to drink as a way of emulating him. The uncle, Mart Quinn, never married, so the disruptive effects of his drinking were never felt at such close quarters.

Billy Quinn certainly identifies Mart Quinn as a root cause of his father's troubles. 'Mart was a very impressive figure and I believe my father admired him so much that he wanted to be like him and that included the drink pattern. I think Dad felt in a way that the drink thing was handed down to him.'

Anita remembers alcohol beginning to have an effect in the home mainly at mealtimes; throughout, Jack's drinking would be confined mostly to the home. Jack Quinn was a smoker but during his drinking bouts he would not bother with tobacco (nor food, either). When the cigarettes disappeared it was a sure sign that the bottle was about to come out again. Anita Quinn: 'Jack would go three or four months without a drink but then it would start again. He always wished he could be like other people and just take a drink with his dinner, but it could not be that way with him. With Jack's problems and Elizabeth's problems, I would get to thinking we were the only family in the world that these things were happening to. I remember going to see a doctor and he told me that I had two crosses to carry. I got really mad at him for saying that. But I knew I had to be strong. I had been pretty determined as a child. These things were happening. I was the one who was there and I was the one who was going to have to take care of it. I would go home and put a good face on it. To anyone else we would look like a nice family but Jack's mother and his family knew what was going on. Sometimes I had to take Elizabeth to school by train and coming back I would often wish that I was on a slow boat to China, that the journey would never end.'

Elizabeth may have been sheltered from many of the worst outbursts of her father's behaviour, but Billy Quinn was at home and directly in the firing line. Once or twice he attempted to leave home because of his father's conduct, and he certainly knew when to disappear from the house, but he stayed on and his own strength of character and early maturity brought him through what could otherwise have been a profoundly scarring experience. Then, as now, he viewed his father's predicament with a mixture of compassion and pain. 'I did have enormous anger at my Dad but mostly there was a feeling of understanding and not wanting to abandon him. You felt the hurt and disappointment every time he started again but I'm sure he felt it too. When he was drinking his actions were desperate. He knew he was going down, he knew everything was going to hell but I think he disappointed himself more than anything. It was bad for Mom. She would come home from work never knowing what she was going to find or if Dad was going to be violent to her. I can remember Mom having to run out of the house because Dad was after her until he got money for another bottle of wine. Dad would run up the street after her. That was awful. Many times it made life hell at home. Money got scarce. We lived on a shoestring and I spent a lot of time at other

people's houses. It was not the situation where you could ever
have visitors in. Later on, it got so we could not keep apartments.
We had to leave California Street as the drinking progressed
and keep moving. My father would get great fits of anger and
violence if he did not get the money to buy booze. He'd get very
loud and the landlords would not take it and we would be asked
to move on. They would say they had relatives moving into the
area just as an excuse to get us out of the apartment. We would
move in the night sometimes because we were going to be
evicted on account of how we did not have the rent. Sometimes
Dad would go into hospital to dry out and he would come back
to a different home. It was a Jekyll and Hyde existence for him.
After two months on booze he would stop and there would be a
rebuilding of life with periods of great togetherness and joy for
us all. Liz did not know too much about the bad times. She was
away at school during the week and Dad was always on his best
behaviour when she was around.'

It was in innocence that Elizabeth first saw the signs of her
father's drinking. She regularly accompanied him to the liquor
store and the visit had childishly enjoyable diversions all of its
own. The store had a promotion for Rheingold beer which
included forms for customers to nominate their candidates for a
Miss Rheingold beauty competition. Elizabeth, who was
thoroughly familiar with the Rheingold brand name from its
presence in the house, would amuse herself while her father
made his purchases, filling in her own entrance form for the
contest she was not yet anywhere near eligible for. It never
dawned on her then that they made many more expeditions to
the liquor shop than to the grocery store:

> In the summer or during other long holidays I remember
> my father drinking with his brother or other friends. They
> would drink all night and in the morning there would be
> bottles and beer stains everywhere. I did not realise how
> much they were drinking or that there was anything
> wrong with it. When Mom would say we did not have
> enough money for groceries I never understood how there
> always seemed to be enough money for beer. I thought

they must have had some special deal with the liquor store. It never hit me that it was not normal. We used to eat a lot of macaroni and oatmeal and I guess that was all we could afford. There was a family of Italians with eight or nine children near our house and they used to give us food. The mother, Mary Esposito, saw the problems we were having.

Family picnics would be accompanied by drink if Jack Quinn was on one of his binges. He would pass out in the car while the young children were left hurt and uncomprehending at his failure to take them to the amusement park as he had promised. On the rare occasions when friends were entertained at home the process had to be undertaken with great caution. Anita Quinn was learning from Alcoholics Anonymous to see alcoholism as a disease, but her children were too young to understand this invaluable and compassionate diagnosis. She did her best to comfort them, sitting Elizabeth and Billy down and explaining that it wasn't their father's fault. On one day when Jack Quinn had taken to his bed with a bottle and Elizabeth was expecting friends to visit, she posted a note on the door which read: 'Go to living room, be quiet, my father has a terrible disease.' At that stage, she says, 'I didn't understand what that meant.'

For Elizabeth there was also the pain when he failed to attend school functions. When every other parent turned up, Jack Quinn would fail to arrive for graduation day. When a father-daughter evening was arranged, Jack Quinn could not make it and Elizabeth had to have a school sports coach as her date. Elizabeth began to dream up fanciful excuses for his absence. The shortage of money in the home could not but affect her also, since most of her friends and contemporaries came from well-to-do families. When the pupils were asked to write an essay on their holiday activities or produce an article for the school magazine, Elizabeth sat down and wrote an account of a family skiing holiday which was the equal of anything her friends had undertaken but which was, in fact, a complete fiction.

If Jack's drinking coincided with school holidays Anita Quinn would organise visits to other members of the family for

herself and the two children and there would be frequent
returns to the Reillys who still lived in Port Jervis. But these
visits only caused further stress between Jack Quinn and his wife
and children:

> My mother would take us to stay with her parents during
> the summer and tell us that Daddy had to stay behind to
> work. Everything was fine there, my grandparents pro-
> tected us and Billy and I looked so good and fit. My
> grandfather taught me to draw and write poems and I got
> more attention from him than I did from my mother.
> My mother was never calm. She was always nervous. My
> father used to come then to fight with my mother and
> make us go home to Connecticut. She wanted to be
> separated from him for a while but he wanted us to go
> back. We would go to meet him at the station in Port Jervis
> and we would be excited but right away there was tension
> between my mother and father. When we got back to the
> house and had a meal my father would be furious. He did
> not like the way the Reillys prepared the food. They were
> very spartan eaters but the Quinns were used to enormous
> amounts of food. My father would go out and buy a whole
> lot of food. Then we would have to go back in a day or two.
> It was going back and forth all the time. We seemed to
> have two homes.

It was only later, as Elizabeth was progressing through her teen
years, that she recognised her father's bouts of drunkenness for
what they were and began to understand the nature of alcoholism. With that knowledge there came times of profound sorrow:

> I began to think I was the cause of my father's drinking. I
> began to think I should not have been born. Later in life I
> could look up to him. He became like a deaf rôle model for
> me. I could see him fighting against alcoholism in the same
> way I was fighting against deafness.

The days of drink were periods of darkness which alternated
with periods which both the Quinn children look back on as a
sun-filled childhood, with a father who accommodated their

every whim. He was generous to a fault when sober, showering them with toys, comics and clothes and was equally generous with his time. It may have been his own way of making up for his inadequacies in other directions but his attentions were none the less appreciated for that. Just as he could always find a few dollars more for another bottle when he was drinking, Jack Quinn could always find the price of another modest gift. His finances were precarious, he never had a bank account but he could always tap the credit union at work for another loan against his wages or borrow from friends, as he regularly did. It was left to Anita to supply life's necessities from her own job in the office of New Haven's largest department store:

> Father was not working regularly so he had all the time in the world for me. He was still a great story-teller and he would always tell stories with lots of dialogue in them. He had a wonderful way of talking. I could feel his voice was deep and strong, very calm and serene.
>
> Dinner time was the most important time at home, when we all sat round the table and talked. My father read all the time and he would tell us about the book he had been reading and I would ask questions about it. At the table Billy and my father would say to me: 'Don't worry, you are not missing anything.' They included me in everything. If I wanted to get on with my food I could go into my own little world and then I would look up and just put my thumb and forefinger together which meant: 'What was that?' It is not the correct sign but it is the sign I always used at home. And then my father and Billy would tell me what had been going on.

There was certainly a defensive mechanism at work here, which Billy Quinn recognised: 'There was a great protectiveness from Dad towards Liz which was a bit too much. Mom was more objective. Dad went through great pain for her. There was so much turmoil in his own life, so much he had to cope with, he saw everything in terms of black and white. It made him more concerned about Liz than the rest of us.'

It was at this time that Elizabeth and Billy Quinn acquired

their lasting taste for show business, through the medium of their local cinema. Billy can still recall his very first visit to the cinema, when Anita took him and Elizabeth to New Haven to see Ethel Merman and Marilyn Monroe in *There's No Business Like Show Business* — a prophetic choice. Billy was just four and Elizabeth was six. Billy: 'We got into that dark cinema, sat down and saw the screen and it was like a new magical life for both of us.' The New Haven cinema was a first-run theatre for new releases; a more familiar haunt for the young Quinns was the Rivoli in West Haven, now converted into a bank. There they became regulars for the Saturday afternoon matinées during Elizabeth's weekend breaks from school. The price of admission was 35 cents and a wonderful afternoon's entertainment including popcorn could be guaranteed for just 50 cents. The Disney films became great favourites. Jerry Lewis was appreciated because his comedy was so visual that Elizabeth could readily understand what was going on. She also appreciated Pat Boone for the clarity of his diction and his dexterity at lip-synching which made lip-reading so easy. The beauty of Natalie Wood, the bubbly cuteness of Doris Day, the strength of Joan Crawford and the vulnerability of Susan Hayward all had their appeal and Billy made sure that Elizabeth understood every nuance. 'I could interpret inside the cinema. We would find seats where I could catch the light coming from the screen and I would turn towards Liz and be sure she could see me signing to her. I would give a literal line-by-line translation all the way through if necessary. I had a high energy level so it did not bother me. I just thought if Liz did not get every word and sense of what was going on then she would not get total enjoyment. I did not want her to be short-changed.'

When she was back at school Elizabeth would describe and act out the story of the film she had seen at the weekend. Her narrative skill made her the centre of attention:

> When I went back to school there would be a group of girls waiting for me and they would sit round while I went through the story of the film I had seen and as Billy had

explained it to me. If it had been an emotional film, I would always cry while I was acting it out. If it had been a musical I could sing in sign language. I had a sense of rhythm and I could get it across to the other girls by movement or by snapping my fingers. They said they could almost hear the music.

Billy often accompanied Elizabeth on her Sunday journeys back to school now that the initial year's hysteria was over. They took a bus-ride to New Haven to catch the train to West Hartford and there was often a long wait at New Haven station. They killed time at a news-stand, leafing through show-business magazines and noting the clothes and hairstyles currently fashionable in Hollywood. After seeing a photograph of Connie Stevens, Elizabeth attempted to adopt her style, with a bubble cut at the front and a pony tail at the back. In due course they graduated from fan magazines to the trade papers, like *Variety* and *Hollywood Reporter*. Their interest was becoming more professional. Which actor was up for which role and was he right for the part?

Elizabeth's school provided film shows with subtitles to help the deaf children. There was one film, *Imitation of Life*, which Elizabeth saw while she was there which struck a deep chord in her. Starring Lana Turner and Sandra Dee, it was a second version of Fannie Hurst's novel of that name, in which the daughters of a fine lady and a black maid grow up together as friends and the half-caste daughter of the maid tries to pass herself off as white in a race-sensitive society:

> That film meant so much to me. I did not want to be an imitation of life. I wanted to *be* life. It made me realise there were two different worlds for me and it made me determined to be a part of regular life.

At the American School for the Deaf, Elizabeth moved on through the junior grades to the equivalent of high school. A new set of teachers took over her education and the syllabus was expanded to include subjects like science and social studies.

There was also Miss Yowell waiting to introduce her young charges to current affairs:

> I had a terrible time trying to learn about world events. Miss Yowell was always lecturing us about how we must read the newspapers and she made it seem so serious and difficult. I could not understand why she never taught us anything about show business or that part of the news. It always seemed to be the bad news on the front page that we had to read and she was so passionate about it she frightened me.

Somewhat to her surprise, however, Elizabeth continued to be one of the brightest pupils in such lessons as English, history and social studies, where her interest was engaged. It was only in the more exact sciences such as arithmetic that she failed to distinguish herself:

> I was always day-dreaming, I never did my homework and I was certainly not a genius but I always got high marks in the subjects I liked. Anything that had an element of story-telling about it was easy for me. I think it was because I had loved my father telling me stories, and I also developed a photographic memory. It trained me to be able to absorb information because we always discussed those stories later. If I seemed to be day-dreaming in class it was probably because I was still going over in my mind what I had just been told. I remember we were taught about the American War of Independence and I was engrossed in it. When we got our report cards and I had high marks the teachers sometimes put an exclamation mark next to the percentage figure. I think they wondered how I had done it. I did find it easy but I also think that perhaps the standards were not all that high and that helped too.

As lessons changed, so did the pupil. The scrawny little child who had been brought to school amid such tears had grown into an attractive young girl with an outgoing personality. Billy Quinn had to reassess his sister when he took her to visit his own school in West Haven and Elizabeth dressed herself up in a fashionable Carnaby Street style outfit of gold mini-dress and black stockings. Billy: 'We walked into the cafeteria and the place went mad. The teenage boys were shouting and wolf-whistling. She set the place buzzing and she walked through it, just floated through it, with great dignity. The next day after that I had more chums at school than I ever had and they all wanted her phone number.'

Within her circle of family and friends Elizabeth was also speaking aloud with freedom and confidence but she had yet to find the courage to risk the voice she could not hear with people she did not know. Billy watched her development without misgivings: 'I guess I worried sometimes for her safety but only as you would for any girl and nothing more than that. If I had to be protective of her it was to save her from any hurt. You know the position and you make sure there are no gaffes. I was happy to make it clear my sister was deaf and I wanted people to take their time, talk slow and let her understand. Most people were very good. They sensed a camaraderie in her. If they could find a way to communicate they would want her for a friend. I could see she definitely had the ability to get on with people. She was more worried about speaking to people than I was on her behalf.'

As Elizabeth entered her teen years, it was Billy who explained to her what it was to have a 'deaf' voice and how it would sound different to other people:

> For years I did not speak to anyone outside school or my family. Friends at school told us of their experiences, when they would speak to hearing people but the people would not be able to understand them or, even worse, they would make fun of their voices. That was a shattering experience for the people it happened to and I made sure it never happened to me. I remember being out somewhere and signing and people made fun of that. It was terrible to be made to feel different. When Mom took me to the store she used to tell me not to sign. She did it to protect me from other children making fun of me. Even though my family said I had a lovely voice it was ingrained in me that deaf people's voices were no good.

I was always scared of speech but I wanted it so much.
I realized early on how gifted Billy was. I would watch
him and he could express himself so well, he had a great
vocabulary, timing and rhythm. I wanted so much to be
like that but I felt I would never measure up. That
coupled with my abhorrence of the hearing world, which
I had developed while at school, and my defences and
insecurity — it was a constant struggle for me. Even very
good friends were surprised that I could speak.

There were occasions at home when Elizabeth would most
certainly raise her voice. Not fully aware of the circumstances
which gripped her parents and brother there, and fortified by
the defences she and her deaf schoolfriends had built for themselves, there were times when Elizabeth would be arrogant,
selfish and stubborn and sometimes all the frustration of her
deafness would boil over. Billy witnessed many of these scenes:
'Liz had problems sometimes. She was full of anger and confusion because she was in the middle of two worlds. She could
see what was going on in the hearing world and yet she was not
part of it. At home she would get in rows and flare-ups. That
anger and frustration would take a physical form. She would
throw things and, damn it, she wanted things to break. I did not
always understand why she had to vent those emotions, why she
had to get so angry. Sometimes I would move in and try to
console her and other times I knew to stay out of it and take a
walk. But without that release she would have gone bonkers. It
was cathartic.'

Billy Quinn's support and understanding, from an early age
and through years of almost continuous crisis, is remarkable and
the value to his sister cannot be over-estimated. Yet it was
achieved without any sense of obligation or sacrifice. He says: 'I
never felt I was being leaned on. I never had any grand vision it
was my job to look after Liz. I never thought about it. It was just
instinctive. I never remember being concerned about what
would happen to Liz in the future. I could see she had a lot more
going for her than many of the hearing girls around. I trusted
her to resolve whatever lay ahead.' As Elizabeth grew to know

above Elizabeth aged 4, New Haven, Connecticut
below Albery Theatre billboards, London 1981

left Elizabeth (6) and Billy (4), West Haven, Connecticut. *below* London reunion, 1982

right First
Lieutenant Jack
Quinn (later of
the New York
Yankees), aged 23.
inset Elizabeth in her
favourite element,
wearing her father's
cap. *below* Anita
Quinn on their
wedding day, Port
Jervis, New York,
22 April 1946

above Mrs Dunn's classroom, 1956
below Elizabeth Quinn visiting pupils of the partially hearing unit at
Knollmead Primary School, Tolworth, Surrey, 1983

more of the events within the family her appreciation of his role deepened:

> My brother had to take on an awful lot of responsibility very early. Billy sure had to grow up fast.

It was a time when each member of the family was being tested as never before. Billy, for example, took on a newspaper round to augment the dwindling finances only to find that even this slender extra income was commandeered to be spent at the liquor store. The endless round of temporary apartments took its toll on all of them and it was not until 1964 that the family was able to settle again with any permanence when they moved into a duplex in West Clarke Street, West Haven.

Elizabeth began now to sense that each member of the family was locked into his or her own personal tragedy:

> We were at rock bottom and our lives were bleak. We were all victims. I was a victim because I could not hear and because I was trapped in two over-protected worlds. Moving between home and school was like moving from one glass bubble to another. I was naive and immature, I knew it, and yet there was nothing I could do about it. My father was a victim of his disease. He did not want to be like that and he was well aware of what was happening. He would try to compensate for it by buying me presents when I got home for holidays and weekends. He wanted to give me something because he felt he had let me down. Billy was a victim of everything that was happening. He was very gifted but he could not go on with his education because there was no money, and because he was at home all the time he had to put up with much more than I did. And my mother was a victim too. She had to try to keep the family going. She did not want anyone to know what was happening to us. She kept reminding Billy and me not to tell people what was going on. So I lied about my home and family. I told everyone at school that I lived in a white house with a white fence and we had servants. I described the conversations I had with my maid and told them that I had horses and rode every weekend. I even took a scrap-book to school with pictures of horses in it and picked out

the particular horse that I rode. I was very convincing. It must have been good training because what is acting but lying and believing in what you are saying?

In the face of these problems Elizabeth began to decline the weekend visits home and would prefer to stay at school to the extent that Anita Quinn would have to write to her daughter pleading for another visit. Elizabeth knew all too well the sort of scene which might greet her on her return to West Haven:

> I remember sitting in the living room with Billy and father would be in the next room in bed drinking. We would be watching television and all of a sudden Billy would tense up. I would ask him what was wrong and he would say he heard the bed creaking and that Dad was getting up. We would sit there scared and waiting. Sometimes Dad would come into the room really drunk and swaying. It was awful. That was why we could never have friends home. We did not want anyone to see him like that.

There were also times of violence though never directed against the children and only once witnessed by Elizabeth herself:

> We were all sitting round the table at dinner. I was eating my meal but, evidently, Dad and Mommy were having a row which I was not aware of. Suddenly Dad jumped up and grabbed the front of Mom's blouse and tore it. It was, in fact, a blouse Mom had borrowed from me and she told him that. He just said: 'I'll buy you a new one.' He sat down again. His face was expressionless.

From the safe distance of school Elizabeth begged her father by letter to change his ways. When Jack Quinn was in Connecticut Valley Hospital on yet another drying-out visit, she wrote: 'Daddy, I'm writing this letter for a special reason to ask you to stay in hospital a little longer so you will be sure of yourself before you come home. Daddy, if you love me, you would do it for me. You see, if you come home and start this again, we'll never want you again and believe me I don't want that to happen. I love you and I miss you so much. Would you do it for me, Daddy, please?' Jack did his best not to let her down but invariably failed.

At school, at least, Elizabeth could isolate herself from the domestic upheavals at home. Her life there was full. She was voted president of her class, of various clubs and of the student council. The annual ceremony of the return of the school football team one year saw her appointed Princess of the Homecoming, a treasured distinction: she was driven around waving regally from a car and decked out in a formal, full length gown and elbow-length gloves. (Not always mindful of her family's financial predicament, she had written to her mother to buy her a pair at $3.99 and send them post-haste. She was astute enough to send that letter to her mother's address at work and added an assurance to Billy that on her day as Princess she was going to *shine*.)

A high-school romance was also underway with a deaf boy named Raymond. It was conducted with some innocence but Raymond's attentions were welcome and valuable not least because he had a car which brought a wider dimension to school life, with dates at restaurants and at the movies. Raymond went on to marry one of Elizabeth's closest school girlfriends. Elizabeth, meanwhile, set about learning to drive and had her own licence at seventeen. The value of being a driver was greatly appreciated later when the isolation and self-sufficiency of night-time driving became almost a therapy to Elizabeth.

Elizabeth was fast approaching the end of her career at the American School for the Deaf. The ease with which she mastered the academic subjects which appealed to her had enabled her to progress through the years as a leading member of the top stream:

> I was clever at school. I had to be to survive. I was one of the best at reading and when we were taken to the library I was always sent to choose a book from the more difficult section. That was because of my father. I could always see the story happening when he read to me and then, just near the end when it was getting really exciting, he would stop and suggest that if I wanted to know what happened I

should finish the book myself. A great many deaf children find reading difficult because they can't get a picture of the words. They know what all the separate words mean but they can't put them together. My father made me so curious to find out what happened in those books that he made me battle on until I won.

In her final year, Elizabeth and her A-stream classmates were entered as a matter of course for an entrance examination which would qualify them for Gallaudet College in distant Washington DC, a college which was exclusively for deaf and hard-of-hearing students. Elizabeth's parents were keen for her to go on to college, where the costs of fees, tuition, books and boarding would be met by a grant from the state's Vocational Rehabilitation fund. Elizabeth had become increasingly restless at school; she was curious to discover what else might be available but she felt no strong ambition of her own to go to college:

> I was bored. My imagination was running wild. I wanted some new adventure. Because I was deaf, my ambition was limited. I did not know yet what I could do. I was just living from moment to moment. I was nervous about going to Washington. I knew it would be a deaf community but it would be a drastic change in my life. I liked the idea of going to a big city where I thought I would be more independent, which I wanted. Half of me wanted that freedom while the other half still wanted me to be taken care of. I had always depended on the people around me and I thought I might fail. I knew it was the end of that part of my life at the American School for the Deaf and there was going to be something more beyond.

The alternative to college was some mundane job which again failed to excite her interest. The money might have been a valuable addition to the Quinn household but her parents never once mentioned that potential advantage to her. Instead, Jack Quinn raised the possibility that her future might lie in becoming a social worker in the deaf world, which would first necessitate a college education:

My father thought being a social worker for the deaf would be a safe field for me. I did not think about it very seriously. I was going by instinct. If I had gone to a boring job like a key-punch operator in an insurance office, which was all the rage with deaf people, I guess I would have got frustrated, I'd have left and just drifted.

She approached the obligatory entrance exam more out of curiosity than with any steely determination to distinguish herself. She knew that the results would come in a fat envelope if she had passed but in a curt note of failure otherwise. She eventually laid her hands on a nice thick envelope and was on her way to Washington.

FIVE

College

Elizabeth left the American School for the Deaf at West Hart-ford with one final but familiar disappointment when her father failed to arrive in time for the graduation-day ceremony. She arrived home to face a summer vacation in West Haven during which the usual domestic turmoil only intensified her insecurity about the immediate future in Washington. For once, even the beach failed to provide its usual comforts and it was a melan-choly summer.

The mood was broken, if only for a day, when Elizabeth and Billy treated themselves to a visit to New York to look round Macy's and walk round the Broadway theatre district. The good-looking girl of nineteen caught many an eye in her lavender mini-dress and matching hat. Billy Quinn recalled that they were happy just to walk past the theatres whose ticket prices were all beyond their reach. Passing one stage door they were startled when the stage doorman suddenly stepped for-ward and beckoned them inside with motions of After You. Billy said: 'We had to explain that we were not part of the show but Liz was looking so good it was almost understandable. Looking back, it seemed almost like a signal of what was to come.'

As she prepared for Washington in that summer of 1967, Elizabeth's excitement at the threshold of a new adventure was swamped by apprehension at what she would find on arrival. When the day came for the eight-hour train journey, yet again Jack Quinn was unable to make the trip and Elizabeth set off with her mother and brother.

Their first taste of Washington made a vivid impact, as they stepped off the train in the main station with its high ceilings decorated with astrological designs and statues and pillars on every side. Their cab then took them through the imposing gates of Gallaudet College to the office where Elizabeth first had to register. There they were directed to her new residence in Peet Hall where she had been allocated a room on the third floor:

> It was a room for two people and it was not as nice as the room I had at West Hartford. My bed was just a metal cot, the room was off a long corridor with a shared bathroom and a shared lounge. The girl I was sharing with was from Missouri and she already seemed intimidated by the place. She was hard of hearing and did not sign. I started to get depressed. I cried when Mom and Billy left. I could not believe that I had made the decision to be in this place. I did not know what to do and I felt very lonely.

It was a solitary existence for Elizabeth for her first few days at Gallaudet until the two-week orientation course for new students began to engage her interest. She met a cheerful girl from Illinois called Ginnie and switched rooms to share with her new friend. Once installed in her new fifth-floor room she found the girls around her better company.

Gallaudet College offered a five-year course leading to degrees in a range of subjects and preceded by a first preparatory year to acclimatise the students to college education. To Elizabeth's delight, the two-week introductory course included a variety show to be put on by the new students when the rest of the college returned from their vacation. The purpose of the show was to give the young strangers an opportunity to get to know each other but it also provided an activity into which Elizabeth could throw herself wholeheartedly. She recalled a story she had read, entitled 'The Gift of the Maji' — a romantic fable about a husband selling the watch he treasured to buy combs for his wife's lustrous hair, while the wife was cutting her hair and selling it to buy a chain for her husband's fine watch. It would make a neat two-hander, just five minutes long. She also plotted a more dramatic short piece about a young girl's suicide as her lover went off with another. As she organised her fellow students into their sketches she began to feel more comfortable in her new surroundings.

The day of the variety show arrived and Elizabeth found herself going on stage for the very first time in front of an audience of nearly 500. She delivered her 'Maji' sketch but was disappointed when her second offering was cancelled through lack of time. The evening ended with awards to the outstanding performers. Elizabeth looked on in disbelief as her own name was signed as the best actress. The first theatrical award of her career was a black mug with gold trim, bearing the Gallaudet symbol.

Despite this triumphant beginning, Elizabeth began to find college life less and less to her taste. Gallaudet offered a wide syllabus, including algebra, geometry, chemistry, physics and biology, but she had neither the appetite nor the ability to cope with such things. Her problems increased when she shone in an early maths multiple-choice test, through sheer guesswork. As a consequence, she was put into the top maths class and once there could not get out:

> I did not go to Gallaudet in a proper frame of mind. I had no real goal. I was not going there for a degree. I went to see what would happen. In subjects like English I thought I could get by but I could not absorb things like mathematics and science. They did not suit my sort of mind which wandered and day-dreamed. They were to do with facts not feelings or emotions which were more interesting to me. I began to skip classes. I spent the time reading or just hanging around. I got notes about not attending, then a tutor was organized to go through the matter with me. I did not turn up to attend the session with the tutor.

The other disciplines of college life soon began to grate. Students had to be in their dormitories by 7.30 p.m. each week night and by 9.30 p.m. on weekends. Male visitors had to be out of the female dormitories by 10.00 p.m. The girls found a secret passage into the building and, covering their absence by stuffing pillows under the bed-clothes, thoroughly enjoyed dodging the curfews. But even with this slight freedom, Elizabeth was still finding Gallaudet something of a disappointment. Outside in the city of Washington there was a printing works which made jobs available to the deaf and America's National Association of the Deaf was based in the capital:

> It was hard to get off the campus. There was a larger deaf community out there but in many ways it was all just like the American School for the Deaf on a larger scale. I began to run a bit wild. I was breaking the rules, breaking the curfews and I got a lot of de-merit marks.

Elizabeth formed a relationship with a student who was two years her senior. He was a flamboyant and amusing character who already had a reputation as a lady's man. He became Elizabeth's first lover:

> He was the first person I wanted to marry. I thought if I gave myself to him in sex then we would be married. There was the curfew at college so we had to make love in a car or a motel room. But he was never faithful to me and he could be mean and inconsiderate. He gave me lots of hard times but also lots of exciting times. When he was having affairs with other girls we would have rows in public. They were very dramatic and I think I secretly enjoyed them. Then we would patch it up again. But I was already nineteen and it was late to be finding out about these things. At the American School for the Deaf we were very prim and thought sex was awful. I had read about sex and making love and it seemed so beautiful but with him it was never quite like that.

Elizabeth's unruly conduct and poor grades through truanting brought a series of unsatisfactory progress reports which did not escape the attention of the Dean of the college, George Detmold, and the Dean of Students, Richard M. Phillips. Towards the end of her first year at Gallaudet, it seemed distinctly unlikely that she would be allowed to return. Her lover came to the rescue with a friend called Frank Turk, who was president of the Junior National Association of the Deaf and also on the college board.

Mr Turk, in confidence, showed Elizabeth her surprising results in the end-of-year examination — 98 per cent. He lectured her hard on her conduct at college then struck a bargain with her: if she promised to work hard in the following year and wrote a letter of apology for her past behaviour, he would help to make it possible for her to stay on. Conveniently, the Dean of Students was away when the reviewing committee met and Mr Turk was true to his word. Elizabeth could continue at Gallaudet but would have to repeat the first preparatory year. That summer vacation, Elizabeth took her first job in the hearing world, a part-time position as sorter in a Post Office in Orange, Connecticut, not far from West Haven. First there was a curious interview with the Postmaster:

> Billy came with me to the interview. The Postmaster asked me questions, I would speak the answer to Billy and then he repeated what I said to the Postmaster. The Postmaster did not understand this and said: 'What's going on here?' It was firmly in my mind that only Billy could understand me and it never dawned on me that the Postmaster could understand me equally well. Anyway, I got the job.

She was paid $60 a week for working 3½ hours a day. Her father drove her to and from work and she had the afternoons free for the beach. The money enabled her to buy clothes and tickets to the movies, but she held back from seeking any contact with her fellow workers and quite happily divided her time between the Post Office and the shore.

There was one particular incident that summer which boosted Elizabeth's confidence. A day trip to New York to visit her Gallaudet lover ended with her catching the last train home out of Grand Central Station and finding the last seat in a crowded carriage among a group of young men. When a drunk stumbled by and fell Elizabeth was the only one to go to his aid and one of the young men in the carriage wrote her a note there and then, saying how kind she was. (He had seen the couple making their

farewells in sign through the train window.) The youth continued his written conversation and by the time he got off at
Westport, names had been exchanged. Dave Miller promised to
be in touch again. Much to the parents' surprise, there was a
phone call to the Quinn household the following Sunday. Jack
Quinn guardedly went to tell his daughter that she would be
having a visitor in an hour:

> Dad was very protective and asked me where I had met
> this boy. He said to be careful. Dave arrived and came in
> and, although I was now twenty, my parents sat right
> there while we talked. He wanted to show me his motor
> bike so we went outside and so did my parents. When he
> was sitting on the bike I saw him glance over my shoulder.
> I guessed there was a car coming and said so. Dave could
> not understand how I could know that, being deaf. Al-
> though it was strange that my parents were there, it gave
> me the confidence to actually talk to Dave and he under-
> stood everything I was saying. This surprised me, that it
> was working and I was able to communicate with him and
> also that he noticed I could be perceptive about things like
> the car coming.

After an hour's conversation another date was set and during
the summer the pair went out to restaurants or the movies. The
first visit to the cinema was a degree awkward as Elizabeth did
not want to seem inadequate and Dave was not sure at first that
she would understand the film. When Elizabeth returned to
Gallaudet they exchanged letters and at the Christmas vacation
she telephoned him, with Billy as usual acting as interpreter. His
mother answered and told Elizabeth that she had done wonders
for her son:

> That again seemed strange to me — that I could actually
> do something for someone else when all my life I was used
> to having people do things for me. It made me feel good
> and I liked it. I wonder where he is now . . .

Much to the surprise of her friends who were sure that her

previous behaviour had disqualified her, Elizabeth returned to
Gallaudet that fall to repeat the preparatory year. This time
Elizabeth was much more ambitious in her plans for the variety
show. She and Billy shared an almost obsessive admiration for
the singer-actress Ann-Margret; Elizabeth had seen Ann-
Margret perform a routine on television using a number of
motor cycles as props:

> There were guys I knew at college with bikes so I borrowed
> four of them. I put three couples on three bikes in the
> background while I got on a big Triumph at the front. I
> was wearing pink culottes, a mauve silk blouse and purple
> boots and I mimed and signed a song called 'Big Time' and
> I got another award. I really enjoyed that.

Billy made the trip from West Haven to see the impersonation.
He arrived to find Washington under siege to the National
Guard because of the riots following the assassination of Martin
Luther King: 'We could hardly get into the college. There was
the smell of tear gas everywhere and soldiers were put on the
campus to protect the students. But Liz was just sensational and
she looked so good. It was the first time I had seen her perform
and it was then that I realized she had really got something.'

Elizabeth's second year at college followed all too closely the
pattern of the first. She was reunited with her lover but still
could not come to terms with the academic effort expected of
her and continued to miss classes, preferring to spend her time
reading or just drifting about. On one occasion an English
teacher took her aside to say that she had a talent which was not
being exploited, but Elizabeth failed to respond to the
encouragement. It soon became clear that she again faced
being sent down at the end of the year and that this time there
would be no second chance.

At home, there was a significant development. Jack Quinn
had been hospitalised yet again for another drying-out period,
but this time he had been contacted personally by Alcoholics
Anonymous. There was to be no over-night conversion but the
positive influence of AA quickly made itself felt and a bond

was forged which salvaged the last years of Jack Quinn's life.

Elizabeth's first knowledge of the breakthrough came second-hand, through letters from home, but she also sensed a new harmony in the Quinn household. She wrote to her mother: 'It was good to hear the news of how Daddy's making out. I really can't wait to get home. My worries are over now that I know the house is full of happy people.' Billy was at home to witness the transformation: 'Some AA members talked to Dad when he was in hospital. They came round to our house and really got involved in our lives. They really cared and counselled us and introduced us to an organisation for the wives and children of alcoholics called Al-Anon. They came into our lives like the Angel Gabriel. There was a regrowth and rebuilding for us all. Sometimes Dad would fall off and go back to his old ways but those people would move right back in again. If ever I saw Christianity in practice, this was it.'

It took time nonetheless for Jack Quinn to sever all connections with drink and some of his lapses were as destructive and alarming as ever. In another letter to her mother, Elizabeth wrote: 'I have been thinking of you and Daddy and Billy ... I wish I was home with you ... The real reason I could not come home was because I knew I would have to invite people in and I did not want them to see Daddy.'

Just as Jack Quinn was gradually emerging, it was stalwart Billy's turn to fall into a crisis of his own. Exhausted by the conflicts at home, he had finally taken as much as he could stand and, in January 1969, he precipitately decided to leave home. His consuming fascination with show business took him to California and the environs of Los Angeles, where he thought he could complete his education and perhaps just possibly carve out some sort of career in Hollywood. This he suddenly set out to do on the slenderest of financial resources.

Billy linked up with a friend and landed in Van Nuys, California, out of touch with his parents in West Haven. For two months, Elizabeth was his sole contact with home, maintaining a correspondence of consolation and support while her brother went through a progress of penury and disappointment on the

West Coast. From their first modest motel, Billy and his pal, both only seventeen, were forced to move on to share a cheap apartment. Their plan to enrol at a local high school was blocked because the young boys were not living with their parents; casual jobs to provide at least a subsistence living proved unattainable.

In his letters to Elizabeth, Billy described the disastrous sequence of events. 'I am not homesick because I do not miss our home. I just miss you and Mommy and Daddy so much. We have so little money that we can't afford to eat so already I have lost 3 or 4 lbs . . . The thing I really miss is Daddy's advice. I wish he was here. I would feel so confident and safe. You know what I mean, Liz, you can always get the right answer from him . . . I really have lost a lot of weight because we have not had a bite to eat in two days and before that one meal a day for two weeks. At least we have instant coffee even though I have to drink it black. It is what's keeping me alive. Whatever you do don't let the family know about it. They would worry too much. We're bound to find something soon, I know it . . . I suppose you will think it foolish but I have the permanent feeling that I will never see either Mommy or Daddy again. In any case, the pictures [you sent] serve as a kind of medicine, if there is such a medicine for loneliness.'

In his second month of absence Billy was beginning to sound distinctly desperate and his friend was about to quit the adventure: 'We have saved up enough for another month's rent but after paying that we are flat broke. So now we are shop-lifters. Mostly we eat in restaurants and walk out without paying. It is so easy and so disgusting. Whatever you do, don't tell Mommy and Daddy . . . What am I going to do? I don't have any money and no room-mate. I'm completely alone. I don't know what to do or where to turn . . . I waited and waited then finally I called Daddy, told him the whole story and asked him if he knew any way out . . . So now I have finally made the only decision I can. I'm leaving California. I hate to admit defeat but in a few years I will come back here to Hollywood and start right out auditioning for film work. I don't know what you want to do when you leave college, Liz, and I don't want to influence you concerning your future, but perhaps you could come back out here with me and we could both work for a career.'

Billy abandoned his West Coast escapade and returned home just in time to join a family support mission to help Elizabeth who had run into troubles of her own. The college authorities had stressed once more that unless there was a decided improvement in her grades she would not be allowed to return after the summer. Elizabeth rang home for her father and Billy to go to Washington to straighten out the latest drama and they arrived bringing Anita with them. Jack Quinn talked to the Dean with soothing effect but it was only a temporary reprieve.

In private, Jack Quinn told his daughter that Anita was deeply offended that she had sent for her father and Billy but had not asked for her mother to help her out of trouble. It was the first time that Anita had raised a protest at her daughter's dependence on her father and Billy while apparently ignoring her, and she remembers it well: 'I just thought if she had a problem why did she not ask for me. After all, I was there the day she was born.'

Inevitably, Elizabeth's career at Gallaudet came to an end at the conclusion of her second year. Few of her current friendships would survive and she would have to leave the safety of a deaf community to go out into the hearing world. It was a prospect she faced with fear and anxiety, but at least there was more cheer to greet her when she returned home to West Haven.

Jack Quinn's recovery was proceeding apace. The lapses into drinking were becoming fewer and briefer and less threatening to the family:

Dad had wanted to stop for so long. Whenever I had come home from school or college and found that my father had been drinking he was always so sorry for being like that. He did not want to upset Billy or me or my mother. It was not the way he wanted to live his life. He wanted to stop drinking and get better. When there was a slip for two or three days my father was so cross; he more than any of us. Billy and I were in the living room one time when my father was on the telephone in the kitchen to the man from Alcoholics Anonymous. Billy interpreted for me what Daddy was saying. He said: 'I started again. I thought I could do it but I can't.' Then he added: 'But when I did drink the glow was not there.' I really think that was the end of his drinking days. But he had to fight all the time. Every day he was fighting to stay off the drink. I saw how he was fighting and how he was overcoming it. We had many long conversations about it and he told me how disappointed he was that it was in his make-up to be an alcoholic. I identified with that. It was in my make-up to be deaf. That was my problem and I was fighting too.

As the drinking problems receded, finally disappearing alto-gether, Jack Quinn, for the first time in fifteen years or more, resumed his role as father in the family. He had to reacquaint himself with his daughter and son and, as Elizabeth was the more vulnerable of the two, she came in for special attention. Without the old tensions, for her first year at home Elizabeth enjoyed herself as the conversations with her father filled in the gaps that had gone unexplained before. She was happy and she was learning.

Elizabeth had returned to her former job in the Post Office at Orange but she soon became bored by her part-time duties there and looked around for a full-time job. She was taken on as a machine operator at Travellers Insurance Company in New Haven. The machine was deemed suitable for a deaf person and though she did not fully understand what it did she soon became efficient at working it. When that became tedious she had herself transferred to a desk job filling in accident reports to be passed on to the claims office.

Her father continued to drive her to and from work and her contact with the colleagues around her was minimal:

Communicating with the girls in the insurance office was a problem. I never spoke. I used to write notes on paper. I never had lunch with them. I went round the shops on my own. I never went out with them although they did ask me. I went to one party and felt very out of place. I left early.

My life was either at home or at the office. I was happy at home and, at that time, I did not feel I was missing anything.

She left the insurance office in April 1970, and took a two-week holiday in Florida with two girlfriends who had a car. For much of the time they drove in bare feet, which Elizabeth still prefers to do today, since it helps her monitor the car's responses.

On her return, at Billy's suggestion, she applied for work at the Barbizon Modelling School in New Haven. Elizabeth was not convinced either of her ability or of her interest in the work but she was provided with occasional jobs as a fashion or photographic model. On one notable occasion, she was chosen as the June Bride to model an elaborate bridal gown to an exclusive audience at a riverside club one Sunday. Jack Quinn drove her there and took his place as the only man in the audience. When Elizabeth strode down the catwalk the audience rose to its feet in applause, asking 'Who is that beautiful girl?' Jack Quinn was able to reply: 'That's my daughter.' No one had even guessed that she was deaf, to Jack Quinn's further pride. After the years of missing her special occasions, he was as proud to be there as she was pleased to have him.

Elizabeth was next recommended to a New York model agency operating from a warehouse on 7th Avenue. She was discouraged when she saw one model reduced to tears by the hardened big-city professionals. She undertook a couple of assignments but missed others, preferring to walk around the city.

It was an achievement to go on my own to New York. I liked the excitement and the energy of the city. I walked round Broadway and Fifth Avenue and saw the fine shops I had read about in *Vogue*. I had my hair done by Jackie Kennedy's hairdresser, Kenneth, with an exclusive room to myself and lots of drapes. I was independent enough to do what I wanted to do in New York but I never had any contact with anyone. I never spoke to anyone.

Elizabeth's contacts were still almost exclusively with her family

and, although she enjoyed their company, this now began to
worry her. She was a young woman in her early twenties,
drifting through a purposeless existence, still over-protected by
her parents and missing most of the experiences that her
contemporaries were enjoying. To try to reclaim some independence she took a lone holiday to Bermuda, refusing even to
be driven to the airport; but that turned out to be a solitary
exercise, apart from the last day when a boy invited her on a
motor-bike tour of the island. It was cheering to be asked but she
still declined actually to speak to him. She fell out of the habit of
her occasional jobs and settled for being a beach bum. An
explosion was building and when it came it was unexpectedly
violent:

> I don't know what started it but I had a blow-up. I was
> screaming and throwing things. I did not believe anyone
> really loved me or truly appreciated me. I was aware I was
> over-protected, that I was different from my friends and
> family. I was at a loss to know what to do. I was still having
> to learn the mechanics of life which I should have learned
> much earlier. If I had been less aware or less intelligent it
> might never have bothered me, but it did and I could not
> accept it. I began to believe there was something deeply
> wrong with me. It was a very dark period. I felt I wanted to
> live a normal life, to be loved by someone and have
> children yet I knew I might not be fully satisfied by that.

The depression was compounded by Elizabeth's poor relations
with her mother at this time. There were misunderstandings
and rows, with Elizabeth as the aggressor and Anita on the
defensive. Anita was still not signing and Elizabeth had difficulty
lip-reading her. Elizabeth was convinced that her mother still
regarded her as a problem which she still did not know how to
cope with. There were long conversations with her father who
worked hard to pull Elizabeth out of her depressed state. He had
his own experience of alcoholism to draw on. When Elizabeth
had lapsed into a silence of several days he drove her into the
country and said to her: 'Don't you know, Liz, I bleed for you.
You hurt your mother and Billy who love you so much. I

understand what you are going through. Nobody knows what it is like to be deaf — except I do, but even I don't know what it is like to be Elizabeth.'

Through these conversations with her father, through self-examination and through wider reading to draw on other people's experience, Elizabeth slowly came to terms with herself and acknowledged that, after all, a little 'study and hard work' might lead her out of her frustrations. She determined to re-educate herself and somewhere in the back of her mind she also sensed that she should direct herself towards the theatre.

Feeling more positive, she applied to enrol at the Southern Connecticut State College in New Haven where she was prepared to tackle the challenge of being a deaf student in an otherwise hearing class. She also applied (twice) to join the summer courses of the National Theater of the Deaf at Waterford, Connecticut. It was not until a year or two later that she learned that both applications had been refused because she had failed to make it clear that she was herself deaf.

There was a more immediate therapy to hand when Elizabeth took up horse riding. Once a week her father would drive her out to a ranch, where she discovered that riding could produce the sort of high that her friends were seeking from drugs or alcohol. She became expert at barrel-racing — a twisting race around a series of barrels — and enjoyed the long rides out into the country. She also bought her own car, a yellow Volkswagen which she christened Cabaret out of admiration for Bob Fosse's film.

In 1971, she was accepted into the Southern Connecticut State College on an 'Introduction to Theater' course, with emphasis on English and literature. She found herself the only deaf student in a class of thirty, and also the object of the attentions of a student who had transferred from nearby Yale University.

His problem was that all his friends were doctors and he had wanted to find a different course. He was also married. He said how much he was attracted to me, how much he

loved me and how torn he was, but I only saw him as a
friend. It gave me some confidence that an intelligent
man could be attracted to me and that he seemed an
outsider too, like me. I had no problems with the written
work and gradually I began to have a feeling of self-worth.
It came very slowly. I still had to be told that I was
intelligent.

It was only in the oral discussions that Elizabeth was frustrated.
She dearly wanted to take part and give her own opinions but
was unable to do so. The teacher had little knowledge of how to
assist a deaf student and Elizabeth had difficulty lip-reading
him, but her ex-Yale friend provided helpful notes.

The course was all theory, without any practical stage demonstration. The students were taken on a tour of Yale Repertory
Theater but there was an establishment even closer to hand
which was to play an increasing part in Elizabeth's life. The
Long Wharf Theater at New Haven, with its open stage and
bustling artistic director, Arvin Brown, has long had a healthy
reputation as one of the outstanding out-of-town theatres on the
East Coast: the focus is on new and contemporary work.
Elizabeth found herself increasingly drawn to the relaxed
atmosphere there and the new experience of live theatre.

She was determined to pursue this new interest independently and would go there on her own, then return to give her
account to the family — a reversal of roles in previous years. She
even made herself a smart theatre-going coat, calf-length in
flower-patterned velvet, and drove herself off to see plays
ranging from *Juno and the Paycock* to Peter Nichols's *A Day in the
Life of Joe Egg* and Strindberg's *Dance of Death*.

I used to take the play and read it on my knee and lip read
the actors. I was amazed at how easily I could follow. I was
fascinated by every part of it, the set, the costumes. At the
interval I would walk round on the set. I would observe the
audience and watch how they would react. I was beginning to learn about audience response. Then I'd go back
and tell Billy all about it. It was a wonderful feeling. I

would be high for days. I desperately wanted to meet the
actors and the theater people but I was too terrified and
too much in awe of them. I once rang up and asked if I
could watch them in a workshop session but I chickened
out of that. I think the Long Wharf was part of bringing
me out of my depression.

As Elizabeth's knowledge and appreciation of theatre deepened
so her tastes changed. She was less now the avid fan of Hollywood, transferring her affections from the American film stars to
the grand ladies of the British stage, notably the late Dame
Edith Evans and Dame Wendy Hiller. It was a change noticed
by Billy and one which left him behind.

At the same time, her choice in reading was changing.
Instead of accepting the books which her father recommended,
she found herself drawn to twentieth-century authors like Fitz-
gerald, Hesse and Hemingway:

> I was interested in the novels which made me aware that
> many of the writers were going through their own depres-
> sions or problems of self-awareness. It made me feel I was
> not the only one, that it was normal to need to know more
> about life. I tried to find out everything I could about Scott
> Fitzgerald and Zelda. I read the letters, biographies,
> anything I could lay my hands on.

She was particularly struck when the British National Theatre
production of *Long Day's Journey Into Night* with Lord Olivier
was screened on American television. Jack and Anita Quinn
were out at an AA meeting so Elizabeth spread the script of the
play on the floor and followed it with the television production:

> My father came home and said 'How was it?' I told them
> how marvellous it was. I described the whole story and I
> had them captivated. I felt so proud that I was able to tell
> them and interest them in something I had seen.

It was only a matter of time before she found a practical outlet
for this recently discovered passion.

SIX

The Turning Point

'Where have you been all this time?', Elizabeth was asked when in 1974 she joined a residential summer course at the National Theater of the Deaf at its headquarters in Waterford, Connecticut. She looked back in surprise at the course administrator, Patrick Graybill. It was not exactly her fault that she had failed to be accepted on her two previous attempts.

Once again, it was time to exchange one world for another — to move from the hearing world back into the world of the deaf. Once again, it had meant leaving her family. This time, Elizabeth had travelled alone, after an emotional farewell. It seemed to her that there had been an unspoken assumption on all sides that this journey was a particularly special one, with implications beyond these few summer months on a theatre course. On the way, she had been wracked with doubts about her ability to re-immerse herself in a deaf community. Would she be able to sign as fluently as she had before?

The warm welcome at Waterford put her at ease, but she had barely had time to take stock when a new friendship blossomed. From the moment she arrived, fellow student Robert McMahon made a beeline for her. This was the start of a relationship which lasted for some years.

First, Elizabeth had to familiarise herself with the National Theater of the Deaf. The NTD was an ensemble group made up of hearing, hard-of-hearing and deaf actors, presenting productions mainly of classic plays given in a stylised sign language accessible to both deaf and hearing audiences. Elizabeth had seen the company both on television and in New York and had been spellbound. Under its founder and director, David Hays, the company had toured the United States and most of the world and won a high reputation. The summer course offered a training in all aspects of the group's work, from mime and movement to signing and stage design. Elizabeth was eager to learn all she could, but she also had a series of adjustments to make. Much of the work was delivered through classroom lessons and she could still not respond in that setting with the necessary concentration. She was also meeting for the first time adults who were securely rooted in deaf culture. They were the sons and daughters of deaf parents or had grown up in thoroughly deaf environments, and were sure of their own identity. Their attitudes and interests differed from Elizabeth's and in some ways she found them a strange and fascinating breed.

The main hurdle came in the workshop sessions of acting, mime and improvisation when individuals would be called on to give their own ideas or demonstrations in front of the rest of the group. Elizabeth could never find the courage to get up on her feet in front of her fellows and restricted herself to passing on ideas for others to put into practice. The acting class run by a sympathetic and encouraging teacher called Alice Spivak, who called the students up in pairs to act out dialogue or scenes from plays, was an exception. She instilled enough confidence in Elizabeth to bring her out in front of the group and to her surprise Elizabeth found, for the first time, that she could actually become the character she was playing. It was an invaluable revelation for her.

As the weeks passed and she became an accepted member of the group, actors from the company told her there was a vacancy in the NTD for a permanent job as wardrobe mistress. They offered to recommend her for the job if she was interested — one over-eager friend went as far as to tell David Hays that she already had previous experience as a wardrobe mistress. Elizabeth, who was skilled at sewing her own clothes, knew that handling stage costumes was something quite different; she hesitated but, under the barrage of encouragement, finally accepted the job. The family were excited at the news, even though the post would take her away for at least a

year. When the summer course broke up, Elizabeth took Bob
McMahon home for a three-week visit. He was welcomed by
the family but Billy overheard Jack Quinn saying to his wife:
'That boy is not husband material.' Elizabeth was displeased:

> As soon as I knew my father felt like that I rebelled,
> swallowed any doubts I might have had and determined to
> stay with Bob.

She returned to Waterford to find that the NTD's first production was an adaptation of S. Ansky's classic Jewish play *The
Dybbuk* — with a large requirement of costumes including capes
and shawls, not to mention the enormous stage backcloths
which had to be sewn together. The working conditions were
unhelpful and Elizabeth found herself plunged into a nightmare
she had not anticipated:

> The man I was working for was a real chauvinist. He
> would toss off instructions, expecting me to know exactly
> what to do and to understand about measurements which
> I never have and never will understand. We worked from
> early in the morning until late at night in a barn with no
> heating. I was freezing and so frightened of this man that I
> would go straight to the designer to check the measure-
> ments instead of asking him. And all this time the
> company was rehearsing and everyone was looking so
> energetic and so happy and there was I sitting at my
> sewing machine feeling as if my whole world had turned
> upside down.

Elizabeth steeled herself to live through this cheerless baptism
into backstage theatrical life and never allowed a note of despair
to enter her letters home. An opportunity arose to vary her
working conditions when the NTD decided to send a separate
company out on tour. It would be a long tour of many months
and many states but she decided anything would be an
improvement on the work at Waterford.

The touring production was a double bill combining *The
Dybbuk* with an entertainment vaguely drawn on the Super-

woman story, called *Priscilla, Princess of Power*. The two plays, with some twenty characters between them, made heavy demands on the wardrobe department. Starting in Rochester, the tour proved a rigorous one. Elizabeth's duties included standing in the wings at each performance preparing the pieces of costume and the props as the actors needed them. She was often too absorbed in watching the actors on stage, learning about their skills and technique, to be able to do her job conscientiously. It was valuable experience for the future but did not lead to full efficiency at the time. One actress rounded on Elizabeth angrily when she handed the actress the wrong hat just as she was about to step out onto the stage.

As they moved from city to city Elizabeth learned quickly that the laundering of costumes after each performance was her top priority. At every date her first task was to go out and find the nearest launderette. In Denver she found it amid the brothels of the red-light district. In Syracuse it involved her in a farcical drama all of her own making. For *Priscilla, Princess of Power*, the cast were dressed in brass-buttoned coloured tops and white trousers. It was an acrobatic piece with much rolling around on the floor: sixteen pairs of white trousers had to be laundered daily and promptly. During the interval in Syracuse Elizabeth was summoned to the men's dressing room:

> I went in and they were all standing in line looking expectantly at me. They were wearing their coloured tops, shoes and underpants — but no white trousers. THEN I remembered I had left the trousers in the drier. My heart just stopped. I turned and ran as fast as I could taking the shortest route to the laundry which was in a different building. I cut through a church which was next to the theater. I went straight through the sacristy into the church and as I raced past the altar I said: 'God, please help me. Why am I always getting myself into situations like this?' I shot down the aisle, past the confessionals and up the stairs into the next building. I grabbed the pants out of the drier, rushed back to the theater and gave them to the actors. Because they had been in the drier too long they had not been ironed and seemed to have shrunk. When the

actors put them on I could see their ankles peeping out
between their white shoes and their wrinkled trousers.

The tour produced its amusing and less amusing incidents for
Elizabeth and it also produced friendships. The leading actress
in the company, who had already caught Elizabeth's attention
at the summer course, was Freda (Fredericka) Norman, a deaf
actress who combined outstanding acting skills with physical
beauty and a warm and generous disposition. She earned
Elizabeth's everlasting gratitude and admiration.

From the earliest moment Freda Norman encouraged Elizabeth to believe that she had a future beyond the wardrobe, that
one day she would make it as an actress. When Miss Norman
went on in *The Dybbuk*, Elizabeth hung on her every word,
expression and movement. She learned every line in the part,
and every night was reduced to tears when Miss Norman sang
her lament to an unborn child over an empty cradle:

> I don't know if she realised how much of an influence she
> had on me but she gave me so much in her acting. After a
> performance I would ask her what she had been feeling
> when she said a line and she would explain exactly the
> reasons for everything she did on stage, how she had to
> position herself so that the hearing actors could reflect the
> emotions she was portraying. She was vibrant. She had an
> aura. Deaf actors express the whole range of emotions
> visually and move their bodies with such eloquence. I
> admired the way Freda controlled her body and her
> emotions. I wanted to be like her but I had no idea if I
> could be a good deaf actress, if I could convey deaf feelings
> in the way that she did.

Another friend was a Swedish hard-of-hearing actress, Gunilla
Wagstrom, who had a more direct, personal influence on
Elizabeth. She was a strong, decisive, free-spirited character
very much in charge of her own destiny, in contrast to Elizabeth's self-doubts and feelings of inadequacy. The two struck up
a close friendship which continued in regular correspondence
when they later went their separate ways:

Gunilla and I talked for hours and for me she was like a walking text-book on self-knowledge. I watched the way she behaved, the way she treated men, her relationships with them, and I was learning all the time. Because Gunilla was hard-of-hearing and because she always had hearing boyfriends, I could identify with her more than with other deaf members of the company.

Despite these friendships, Elizabeth was not entirely popular within the company. Because she was from the different background of a hearing family, because her interests had expanded beyond the deaf world to conventional movies and literature, she was treated with suspicion and sometimes hostility by some of the members. Billy had once told her that though she was deaf physically she was not deaf culturally: the wisdom of that remark was being brought home to her. She was being exposed for the first time to the inward-looking, self-sustaining culture of the deaf, presumed that this was where she belonged and yet could not become part of it or even feel any connection with it. It was an irony that she was one of the most profoundly deaf people in the group and yet with that very basic common denominator still could not be accepted into their world:

It was a very lonely feeling. I knew that whatever I was going to do, I was going to have to do it alone.

In compensation, Elizabeth felt a growing conviction that the stage was where she belonged and she began to commit herself to the idea of becoming an actress:

I loved the smell of the stage, the smell of the powder the actors used to whiten their hair, I loved the glitter of the costumes and the stage lights. I loved seeing the audience out there, even though from the wings I could only see the front three rows. I watched the actors all the time and began to feel that I could do it. This was something I wanted to do, something I needed to do and almost something I knew I had to do.

When the company first arrived at Syracuse University, scene of the trouser episode, Elizabeth suddenly realised that this was where her father had played football. It brought her a rare feeling of proximity to her father, as though she could feel his actual physical presence. These pleasant thoughts were rudely dispelled by the chaos awaiting the touring players. The theatre was closed, and while the crew set up in a church hall Elizabeth had to organise the costumes from classrooms elsewhere in the university. It was early evening by the time she finished her many tasks and the disruption had lowered her spirits far enough to convince her that she would never get beyond being the harrassed wardrobe mistress in a company only part of which she could claim as friends. As she walked into the church hall, with the setting sun shining through tall arched windows onto the polished floor, a movement at the far end of the hall caught her attention:

> I saw a figure walking by and there was something about the walk that touched me but I did not know what it was. Then the figure turned round. It was my father. He was there. I ran to him and he picked me up in his arms and twirled me round. It was just as if he had come to rescue me. He said that the crew did not seem very nice and I told him they were making me unhappy. He led me downstairs and there was my mother waiting. I was so happy to see them both. My father took me by the arms and said: 'Elizabeth, the hardest thing in the world is patience. The hardest thing is waiting your turn but, believe me, your turn will come.' When he got home he wrote to me and said: 'I am very proud of you and what you are doing even though I can't understand why you want to. Remember, the same God who gave me a new life is also helping you ... You make my life worthwhile.'

The Quinns had been to New Hampshire for an Alcoholics Anonymous convention where Jack Quinn had been guest speaker. They had stopped off at Syracuse to surprise Elizabeth. Since his recovery from alcoholism Jack Quinn had devoutly embraced the Catholic faith: he saw the hand of God in his renewal and, beyond this, in the world about him. When he

shared with Elizabeth his experience of religious conviction it
struck a chord within her. Never were father and daughter so
united, so fulfilled in their companionship and, quite simply, so
adoring of each other:

> When my father was describing the beauty and power of
> God's Creation there was a glow about him. I could see
> that he had found an inner peace. I felt so lucky, so blessed,
> that such a man was my father. Even though I had had a
> nightmarish life with this man, his honesty, his integrity,
> his courage, his love and his understanding were all gifts
> to me.

Strengthened by her father's encouragement, Elizabeth completed the tour. Afterwards she visited Washington to see her
boyfriend, Bob McMahon. When she returned home, un-
settling news awaited her. Her father's throat had been
troubling him and he was booked into the hospital for a
complete check-up:

> It was, supposedly, a minor thing but something did not
> register right in me. He had been in and out of hospital so
> often when he was drinking that there was no reason to feel
> alarmed. But I did.

Elizabeth returned to the NTD and her father went into
hospital, where he was kept for further tests. Elizabeth took time
off work and returned to West Haven where her mother told her
that an ulcer had been diagnosed and an operation might be
necessary. Elizabeth went straight to the hospital where she
found her father in a drowsy state but pleased to see her. He
described the tests, then added: 'I heard the word malignant.'
Elizabeth tried to persuade him that he had misunderstood but
the impact of that single word was not lost on her.

She returned home and said nothing of this to her mother.
Jack Quinn came home within a few days and for a further
month the precise nature of his illness remained uncertain.
Elizabeth returned to Waterford in the meantime. On her next

visit home she arrived with a new hairstyle which had streaks running through her dark hair. The family were all in the kitchen with Jack Quinn standing by the washing machine with his hands in his pockets. There was a light conversation about the new hairstyle until Elizabeth sensed a strange atmosphere in the room. She asked what was the matter. Jack Quinn took her into a corner and said quietly: 'They have confirmed that it is malignant.'

> It was the most awful thing that had ever happened to me. I could feel the tears coming but my father grabbed me by the arms with both hands and sat me down in a chair and said: 'Elizabeth, all the crying in the world will not help. What we must do is accept whatever is God's will.' Then he looked away from me and said: 'As a matter of fact you would be better off without me.' I was stunned. I just could not understand what he meant. I stared at him not believing what he was saying. It didn't make any sense to me at all — not then. Later, I understood it. But not then.

A malignant growth had been confirmed on the oesophagus. It was small and there was a choice between operating then or waiting until it really bothered him. The family doctor advised against the operation but Jack Quinn decided he would prefer to get it over with.

The operation was set for 15 January. Well in advance of that date Elizabeth and Billy went to see the surgeon who would be performing the operation. He explained the details of the operation and said that their father had a 90 per cent chance of recovery as he was in good physical shape. Jack Quinn continued to visit the hospital for tests and Elizabeth thought that he looked the healthiest person on the ward.

On the Sunday before the operation Elizabeth and her father fell into a long conversation in the living room at home:

> There were just the two of us. He was sitting in a chair in the corner and at first I was sitting on the couch and then I

moved on to the floor near him. We talked for about three or four hours. We were talking about faith. He explained to me how he had shunned God and the church and how his life had been all messed up and how in the last five years he had come back to God and he had never felt so right or so much at peace. At that time I was confused about who or what to believe. My father said to me: 'Elizabeth, don't let anyone tell you what to believe or who to believe. You will find it your own way. You will know when it is right for you, even if it takes a long time. Live a day at a time.' He put his finger and thumb very close together and said: 'Life is that big. It is not worth becoming upset about things. It is very hard to understand that, but work on it. Just keep looking at life and experiencing it to the full. That is what it is all about.'

Jack Quinn was admitted to hospital the next day. Billy went to visit him and his father gave him instructions about what to do with the family in the event of his death. Billy pleaded with him to stop but he gave every sign that he did not expect to last long. He had already told a priest: 'I would love to stay but if He wants me to go then I have never been more prepared.'

On the day of the operation Anita, Elizabeth and Billy were at the hospital at 6.00 a.m. to see Jack before he went into the operating theatre. The surgeon came to see him and asked him if he was ready. He replied: 'Yes. Are you ready? Then we will make a good team.' He was given an injection and the family was allowed to sit with him while the anaesthetic took effect. As Jack was wheeled into the operating theatre, his parting words were: 'See you in a while.'

The operation was expected to last seven hours and the family were advised to go home rather than wait in the hospital; if the hospital had not contacted them within seven hours, then the operation was successful. Billy went to work and Elizabeth and her mother went home. They broke the long, tense wait by driving to the beach; it was cold, so they sat in the car and stared at the water. They returned home and when the seven-hour deadline arrived telephoned the hospital to be told that the operation had been successful. They were invited to visit but

were warned that he was in an intensive-care ward. Billy had
already been warned by his father that the family should not
make any visits to intensive care as it would be too upsetting for
them, but none of them could stay away. When Elizabeth and
her mother arrived at the hospital Billy was already there. He
had already seen his father being taken out of the recovery room
and reported that he had looked grey and very pale but
otherwise the same. The three of them waited in the hallway,
then Anita let Elizabeth and Billy go in ahead of her:

> My father was in terrific pain. He had no clothes on, just a
> sheet covering him and there was this great big bandage
> on him and I could see blood stains round the bandage.
> There was a wonderful nurse there who was a friend of my
> father's and she said: 'He's all right. He is just uncomfort-
> able.' She said she would ask the doctor if she could give
> him some more morphine. My father was strapped down
> to the bed. After the nurse had given him some morphine
> he calmed down a bit. I picked up his hand and he spelt
> 'Hi' with his fingers. Then he spelt 'Where's Mommy?' I
> could not believe it. Even though he was in great pain he
> still managed to do that. Billy was standing next to me and
> suddenly he started to fall. He was absolutely ashen. He
> said: 'I can't take it.' I grabbed Billy and we walked out of
> the room. I said to my mother: 'He asked for you.' She
> went over to him. Outside in the little waiting room both
> Billy and I broke down and cried. While we were sitting
> there I was looking at the swing doors into the intensive
> care unit. There were two little windows in the doors,
> covered with glass with a kind of wire mesh in the glass
> making squares. I could see my mother through one of
> those squares. She was standing by my father's bed hold-
> ing his hand. I saw her bend down and kiss him and I saw
> her saying something to him. Looking at them together I
> saw the strength of their love. I thought how it had been
> my mother who supported my father that day when they
> first left me at the American School for the Deaf and how
> she had supported him all through his drinking years.
> Now, in his pain, she was supporting him still.

The family were allowed just five minutes with Jack Quinn each hour. Finally they became so tired that they went home to sleep. The next day he was sitting up in bed with an oxygen mask on his face and the family were told that he was making an amazing recovery. Hopes soared. Elizabeth and Billy took a drive in the evening until Elizabeth decided out of the blue that they should turn back and find out how their father was doing. Billy called the hospital from the telephone in the kitchen. The news was grave. Jack Quinn had had a relapse:

> We rushed to the hospital and again Mommy let Billy and me go in first. The doctors were all around him and he was on a life-support machine. The doctors said they were trying to save him but he was paralysed from the neck down. They told me to speak to him: 'Talk to him. He can hear you.' I screamed in his ear: 'Daddy, I love you so much. Please don't go away from us.' I looked up at his heart machine and it was not regular. Then my mother came in. The doctors left. For the next hour I sat with my father by myself, holding his hand, watching him and praying hard. He had such wonderful, powerful hands and I was holding onto them.

The family had to wait outside while the doctors again grouped round the bed. When they emerged, they said that Jack Quinn had died five minutes ago:

> The nurse came out and I asked if I could go back to see my father. I wanted to hold him. I wanted to be with him. I felt that this could not be the end. Not yet. When he stopped drinking I had got to know him and he was so wonderful. We were the best of friends and he had been so full of life. The nurse explained that they did not really know what had happened: 'He was doing remarkably well and then all of a sudden it was like some force was dragging him away from us and we were trying everything to bring him back. But there was some power behind him pulling him away. He was a very special person.'

The rest of the family went downstairs and left Elizabeth alone in the waiting room. She sat there feeling nothing but emptiness

until an aunt came to say that Billy had disappeared and she
feared he was on the verge of a breakdown. It was now 2.00 a.m.
and the hospital seemed deserted apart from a few night nurses
on duty. She searched the many floors and finally found him
sitting on a bench in a deserted waiting room. He was crying:

> That was like another body-blow to me. Billy had always
> been such a tower of strength. I stood there and watched
> him for a few minutes. Then I went to him and he said: 'I
> don't know what I am going to do.' We stayed there for a
> while, talking.

It was 4.00 a.m. when the family got home to try to sleep.
Elizabeth was on the couch and Billy on the floor. Within an
hour, Elizabeth woke up and walked into the kitchen to find her
mother sitting there:

> It was strange, as if she had willed me to wake up. She said:
> 'Elizabeth, I want to talk to you. I know that it is very, very
> hard for you and Billy. Daddy has done his duty on earth.
> It is God's will. We must carry on by ourselves but,
> Elizabeth, I can't do it alone.' For the first time in my life I
> realised that I had to try to support her. I was being asked
> to give emotional support to another member of my
> family. That had never happened to me before.

On the day of the funeral, the house in West Clarke Street was
filled with Jack Quinn's friends from the railroad and from
Alcoholics Anonymous. As her mother introduced her father's
work colleagues Elizabeth recalled them from her father's
accounts of events at work and was struck by the accuracy of his
descriptions:

> I do not normally like wakes or funerals. I do not really
> approve of them. But my father was absolutely beautiful in
> the casket. He looked exactly like himself, completely at
> peace, as though he was sleeping. Looking at all the people
> there I realised just how much my father had done in his
> life.

Anita Quinn had maintained a perfect calm and control throughout the last illness and death of her husband. It was a year before the full impact of his loss truly hit her but friends were in the meantime worried about her apparent composure. Elizabeth and Billy discussed the future with her. Elizabeth had been told by the National Theater of the Deaf that if she chose not to return they would fully understand. Anita Quinn told her children: 'I don't want you to worry about me. I will be all right. It is important that you do what you must do.'

SEVEN

Chicago

Elizabeth returned to the National Theater of the Deaf in February 1975, suppressing her grief with great effort. Inevitably it surfaced from time to time, bringing back all the insecurities which she had just begun to conquer. When an NTD bus failed to wait ten minutes for her boyfriend, Bob McMahon, she took it as a direct personal slight; it was the same when an attack of bronchitis had her coughing in the wings and disturbing the audience, and she was repeatedly told to be quiet. She became suspicious of those closest to her, even her good friend Gunilla. She felt that her mother and Billy were bonded together and that she was rejected by them as an uncared-for outsider. She even questioned the relationship with McMahon, doubting that he had any real commitment to her.

He, in fact, was the first to come to her side when she rejoined the NTD tour at Lake Placid, New York. Elizabeth was asleep in her hotel room, unable to hear the banging on the door, and McMahon had to dismantle the lock to get in. He stayed with her for part of the tour, which she genuinely appreciated. When, after a discreet interval, Freda Norman and others in the company asked her to tell them about her father's death, she could see that their sympathy was sincere.

But these were interludes in a period of overwhelming despondency. Elizabeth was making more and more mistakes in her work for the company. In conversation with her colleagues she was awkward and her remarks often misunderstood, which further reduced what little rapport there was between them:

> Looking back, I think many of these problems were self-inflicted. I believe that for a person to grow and become

aware of themselves they have to experience the worst pain and to make their mistakes. Without knowing what I was doing I believe, deep down, that I chose to do these things. I knew I had to tear apart the web that the circumstances of my life had created around me. I had to take all those threads apart and weave myself a new tapestry. That was what my father had been trying to tell me when he said I would be better off without him. I did not understand what was happening at the time but actually it was the turning point of my life.

The immediate effect was that she lost her job. It was mutually agreed that she was not cut out to be a wardrobe mistress but she was allowed to take part in the work of the company to see if she had the potential to become an actress in the National Theater of the Deaf. The first test came when a director arrived from New York to take a week's experimentation with the company to build up to a new production for the next season:

> I so much wanted to be a member of the NTD but I just could not do it. They were doing improvisations based on children's stories and fairy tales. Everyone sat in a circle with the director and took it in turns to get up and try things out as the ideas occurred to them. It was terrible. I was totally impressed with their creativity. I had never seen anything like it. Then someone said: 'I understand you are part of this company. Let's see what you can do.' I froze up.

When Elizabeth did manage to get to her feet in a group session, one of the actors turned on her and said: 'This is not for real, you know. We are only acting.' Fortunately Freda Norman witnessed the put-down and walked over to tell the actor: 'She was only acting.'

> If Freda had not come to my defence I would have clammed up again and said to myself: 'Oh God, that's another thing I've done wrong.' But I felt I had achieved something. If I appeared to be doing it for real, well, that is what acting is all about, isn't it? Maybe I could do it.

Sometimes when people say unkind things it can spark you off. That is what that incident did for me.

Elizabeth survived the week and, at the recommendation of Freda Norman, was invited to join the NTD's five-week summer course as a participating actress.

Not at all cheered by the events of the experimental week, Elizabeth summoned up her courage to give a better account of herself at the summer course. She prepared herself mentally and physically to make the best possible impression on the company, but apprehension was beginning to creep in when she arrived at Waterford. She was tripped at the first step when an NTD member asked if it was true that she was suing the company over her dismissal as wardrobe mistress. It was a rumour that had been circulating, and it had no foundation, but Elizabeth interpreted it as further evidence of the resentment against her within the company. For the rest of the course she was fighting a losing battle against the bitterness she felt was directed towards her:

> But I started work. Improvisation again, sitting round on chairs in a circle. Five weeks of agony for me. Every time I got up with an idea I would turn hot I was so frightened. I would explain my ideas and then ask: 'Do you think that is any good?' I was really begging for approval. It was pathetic.

Elizabeth resisted the daily temptation to quit and made her occasional contributions to the exercises. They tended to be low-key as she was given the smaller parts and then usually hid herself behind her long hair. Then she was given the dominant role in a two-hander by Strindberg, in which two women meet as strangers on Christmas Eve.

Freda Norman stepped forward, taking pins from her own hair to pull back Elizabeth's tresses and fix them with her face revealed. With no place to hide, Elizabeth went up to take her position:

I really did not know if I could do it or not. We started and, to my astonishment, out of nowhere, emotion came and took over and I went through my lines. At the end there was absolute silence and then slowly, one by one, the members of the company came up and congratulated me. It was a wonderful feeling to have won the approval of the company at last.

She went home that night and wrote in her diary the two words: 'Tasted triumph.' It was a short-lived victory as two days later NTD director David Hays told her that he did not think she was yet ready to join the company as an actress. Elizabeth, in honesty, could not disagree. The five weeks invested in the course were not without dividends. The experience of watching the actors at work, responding to each other's ideas and sometimes trying to outwit each other in improvisations, had been usefully absorbed. She had also met a girl called Barbara Lind who was going to Chicago to set up a Children's Theater of the Deaf: Elizabeth was invited to join the project. It was an offer of $120 a week to present stories and poems for children in both deaf and hearing schools. Elizabeth said she would think about it and let her know. She left the NTD with mixed feelings of great sadness, gratitude that she had managed to see the course out and no little relief that it was over. Her plan was to join Bob McMahon in Florida, but first she drove home to West Haven, pausing at the beach to sit on the sand and look out to sea in quiet contemplation of the direction life was taking her before going to the house in West Clarke Street. It was one of the very few, fleeting visits she made home for the next year or so.

When Elizabeth joined Bob at Daytona Beach, Florida, they found they each had a proposition for the other. Elizabeth told him of the invitation to set up the children's theatre in Chicago and suggested he join her. He had just finished college and had taken a job in Daytona keeping the local palm trees in trim, but was interested in the move north. His own proposal was that the two of them should take an apartment and live together. Elizabeth's first thought was for her mother's reaction but she

resolved to take this major decision on her own and agreed to
the idea. They found an apartment, furnished it with a few
personal touches and between sessions of swimming and surfing
Elizabeth began learning to cook — with only mixed success
and sometimes messy failures.

Despite her new home base, it was a travelling summer of
long car drives as she shuttled between Daytona, Washington,
New York and West Haven. In New York she went with her
friend Gunilla for a rendezvous with Gunilla's brother, who was
booked to arrive at the plush St Regis Hotel. The brother failed
to appear and the two girls, both almost penniless, spent the
night trying to sleep on the deep pile carpet of the ladies'
washroom until they were ejected by the police. Elizabeth and
Bob went to Washington for a World's Federation of the Deaf
convention where the NTD was giving a performance, and
Gunilla was again there. Gunilla was returning to Sweden, so
Elizabeth had to say farewell to her best friend who had
supported her through her years with the NTD.

Long, inter-state drives were to become a feature of Elizabeth's life. The first, and most alarming, took place that summer
when she set off in her VW from Daytona to drive to Washington. The southern states had seen violent race riots that year and
Bob gave her instructions to ring him when she had passed
through Georgia and reached the safety of South Carolina.
Elizabeth set off in the early evening and enjoyed an un-
disturbed drive. Once she was beyond Georgia she pulled up at
a truck stop to find someone to help her to make the telephone
call. It was approaching midnight, the place was full of truck
drivers and Elizabeth was wearing a short denim skirt and a
flimsy top. No sooner had she reached the counter than one of
the truckers started making clumsy advances towards her. She
decided to get out fast but he followed her. Elizabeth went to her
car and the driver climbed into the biggest truck she had ever
seen. She decided to sit and wait in her car and eventually the
truck pulled out and left. Elizabeth waited a further ten minutes
for safety, then continued her own journey. A few miles along
the otherwise deserted highway she saw the truck parked on the

side of the road and passed it by. The next time she saw it, it was in her rear-view mirror:

> The lights were going from one side of the road to the other as he came nearer and I knew I was being followed. I stepped on the gas and hoped my little car would be all right. The headlights were getting brighter as the truck came up behind me. The chase went on for fifteen minutes, then he started to come alongside me. I was sure he was going to try to push me off the road. The wheels of the truck were so enormous that they towered above my head as we raced along side by side down the highway. Then, to my surprise, he passed and slowly drew away and out of sight. I took my foot off the gas. It seemed somehow symbolic to me. I had been threatened but I had handled it.

By the end of the summer Bob McMahon committed himself to going to Chicago with Elizabeth, on the understanding that he could audition to join the children's theatre when he arrived. The two of them set off in the loaded VW for a midnight arrival in Chicago and a warm welcome from their new landlady. McMahon was accepted without audition, but they had arrived too early and rehearsals were not scheduled to start for another month. They had time to establish themselves in their new home with Elizabeth taking on the responsibility of running the apartment, shopping for groceries and other essentials and making the rounds of the garage sales to pick up oddments of furniture. They were routine chores but she was conducting them herself for the first time. As the children's theatre would only occupy them for two days a week, Bob took a job in a department store and also found employment as a model — Elizabeth accompanied him, to lip-read the photographers and interpret for him.

The Children's Theater of the Deaf was to be a four-person unit with two deaf actors and two professional hearing actors who would be the voices of the deaf pair as well as making their own contribution. When rehearsals started they set out to evolve a 45-minute long programme of poems, stories and songs which they would take out to the schools around Chicago and Illinois.

Among the poems they worked on was 'You Have To Be Deaf To Understand', by the deaf poet, William Madsen. They decided to perform a short sketch before each verse to illustrate what was to come. Elizabeth put forward her own idea for the last verse; it was approved but she was told to act it out on her own. The sketch was set on a racecourse, where a frail old lady triumphs over a pompous rich man standing next to her at the Tote: the broken-down no-hoper which the old lady has bet on beats the favourite and she goes home with a sackful of money. Elizabeth was told to go home to work on the scene and present it to the group the next day. After a sleepless night and precious little positive thought she arrived for the following day's session:

> The rehearsal started and we were getting closer and closer to the sketch. I was getting more and more fright-ened. Finally, there I was standing up by myself with everyone sitting round watching and I just burst into tears. I thought: 'I can't do it. Daddy, please help me.' The director said it was not a test, that we were all working together and not to be afraid. He was determined I should do it so I thought I might as well get it over with. I played all the parts of the man, the old lady and the two horses and as I did it I could not believe what was happening because everyone in the room was laughing and laughing. At the end there seemed to be a sparkle everywhere. They all hugged me and I was crying with happiness. It was my first real breakthrough in an improvisation.

Other entertainments devised for the young audience included Bob and Elizabeth paired, respectively, as Winnie the Pooh and Rabbit, and an enactment of a story called *The Red Balloon* in which McMahon was a little boy and Elizabeth the balloon, his best friend. She looked forward to the day when she would be applying for a serious role and would list among her credits such impressive past performances as Rabbit in *Winnie the Pooh* and Balloon in *The Red Balloon*. The sillier aspects of her work did not escape her and more than once she found herself swallowing her pride to commit herself to another childish endeavour. But there was also the reward of the open enthusiasm from the children at the performances. The group received a flow of letters asking for return visits.

There was one poem in the programme which Elizabeth thought somewhat advanced for the youngsters. It ran:

They say I'm deaf
These folks who call me friend
They do not comprehend

They say I'm deaf
And look on me as queer
Because I cannot hear

They say I'm deaf
I, who hear all day
My throbbing heart at play
The song the sunset sings
The joy of pretty things
The smile that greets my eye
Two lovers passing by
A brook, a tree, a bird
Who says I haven't heard?

Aye, tho' it might seem odd
At night I oft hear God
So many kinds I get
Of happy songs and yet
They say I'm deaf.

When I did that poem for the kids, at first they were restless but I was able to capture them. On the line, 'The smile that greets my eye', I pointed to one boy and he was smiling. The kids beside him looked at him and I knew they were with me and the feeling I had given them something filled me with joy.

The Chicago Children's Theater of the Deaf may have been one of the smaller theatre ensembles around but in its way it was also a microcosm of all the other theatre companies. It had its own frustrations and tensions, reflected in Elizabeth's letters home at the time:

> The hearing actors seem to be the stars of the group — and this is the Chicago Theater of the DEAF ... The theater is such a rough business. I'm constantly fighting for my rights as a deaf woman in the Chicago Theater of the Deaf. These are experiences that I will have to confront or battle through and I will.

The contact with hearing actors, the fact that the group played to hearing children as well as deaf and regularly met their hearing teachers, produced a new need in Elizabeth. Despite the fact that the only people she had spoken to during her years with the NTD had been members of her family, she now wanted to find the confidence to talk to the hearing people with whom she was increasingly coming into contact. She began a course with a speech therapist, Sandy Sherizen:

> I wanted to reach out and speak to the people I was meeting. I wanted to do more than be a deaf actress. Sandy could sign as well and the lessons she taught me were invaluable. She showed me where to put my tongue for certain sounds. When she demonstrated a technique it all seemed so simple. After years of struggling, it was falling into place: the difference between the *ch* and *sh* sound, the difference between *t* and *d* and the fact that in some cases *ph* is the same as *f*. And the hardest one of all was the *str* sound. She also taught me more about lip-reading and how by watching the muscles round the mouth, nose and even the eyes — as well as the lips — you could tell what people were saying. Those lessons were a revelation but it still took me a while before I found the nerve to put them into practice.

Elizabeth was one day taken by surprise when a colleague who was helping her to make a phone call suddenly placed the receiver in her hand and told her to speak into the mouthpiece. He would then listen for the response and interpret it to her:

I spoke into the phone but I was sure my friend would have to interpret what I was saying again to the person I was calling. To my amazement, he didn't. I was astounded that I had been understood. It was the first time I had used the phone myself.

Another development in Elizabeth's life in Chicago was her acquisition of a tele-typewriter — a significant boon which she has used ever since. Known as a TTY, it is a machine into which a telephone handset can be plugged. With a keyboard for sending messages and a screen for receiving messages, both transmitted by the same impulses as a telephone, it operates like a Telex machine and enables a deaf person to have a conversation without being interpreted by a third party:

Hitherto I had always had to find someone to help me with the phone and it was always so frustrating. Even Billy, who was a marvellous interpreter, was not as good as being able to use the TTY myself.

But while outwardly Elizabeth was succeeding in her new job and developing fast as she went along, there was turbulence on several other fronts. The relationship with McMahon was deteriorating. They both had their own individual sets of problems to work out and in doing so they were giving less to each other. Elizabeth's own problems were coming very quickly to the fore.

They started with a series of physical pains, first in her eye then in her left breast, which her doctor attributed to nerves. It was just over a year since her father's death and she was feeling increasingly guilty that she had abandoned her mother and Billy since that time. She was having financial problems sustaining herself in Chicago and knew that Billy and her mother were facing the same in West Haven where Anita Quinn had been forced to sell the car. The cumulative effect brought her into a deep depression. She told her speech tutor of her problems. The tutor recommended her to a well-known psychiatrist in Chicago and after one meeting the psychiatrist proposed that she start

a course of sessions with a junior therapist, Sue Goldstein.
The first meeting was not a great success. The therapist
wanted to explore why Elizabeth felt she had been dumped on
her, and that was not an important issue for Elizabeth. But, over
a year of twice-weekly visits, Sue Goldstein became an important figure in Elizabeth's life and development:

> Sue was the best thing that could have happened to me. It
> was difficult at first but she was very patient. She would
> never give me answers; she would make me delve into
> myself to find my own answers. It was the first time I had
> been made to think for myself instead of accepting what
> others were telling me. It was hard and there were times of
> silence when I was too afraid to find the answers. She made
> me think deep down about things in the past — the anxiety
> as a child of going back and forth to school, my father's
> drinking, my mother not learning to sign and not being
> able to communicate, my failure at Gallaudet when I had
> no discipline or responsibility, why I felt so unloved. It was
> all the anger and frustration that was repressed or had not
> been constructively expressed. She made me discuss my
> hearing-loss problem and why I would not use my voice.

Sue Goldstein had a limited ability in sign language but during
their sessions she insisted more and more that Elizabeth should
use her voice. This began slowly with Elizabeth first making her
responses vocally then stopping to repeat them in sign. It also
led to outbursts of anger from Elizabeth:

> All the way through Gallaudet and at the NTD I had not
> spoken to anyone except my family. But Sue was after me,
> pursuing me, urging me to use my voice and not just with
> her. She was always asking if I talked when I went
> shopping the day before, had I been speaking at the
> schools we went to. I hated her asking me those questions
> and I used to get mad because the answer was always No.
> That is what made me angry. I wanted the answer to be
> Yes. I wanted to go out and speak but I still was not brave
> enough. Sue said my problem was really a hard-of-hearing
> problem but that I was deaf. I desperately wanted to reach
> out and be intelligent with people.

The therapist introduced Elizabeth to a powerful exercise in which she placed an empty chair in front of her, told her that the chair was occupied by herself (Elizabeth) at the age of eight or nine and guided her into having a conversation with her younger self. Elizabeth could not enter into the exercise at first but was gradually persuaded to undertake it. It revealed at least one piece of information that had remained buried in her subconscious for years — that for a short time her parents had once been separated:

> I remember arriving home from school by train and being met by my mother at the station. When we walked down the station steps there was Daddy waiting in the street. I could not understand why they were arguing. My mother said: 'Come along Elizabeth, we are going home.' My father said: 'Would you like to stay with me. We will go out for something to eat.' I was between the two of them. They were both holding my hands, literally pulling me in different directions.

The exercise also uncovered to Elizabeth the child/woman conflict within her. She came to see that every time the woman that she had become tried to take a step towards adult maturity, the child that she still was clung on to the dependencies which prevented her living her own life:

> In an acting class one day I had to play a scene to an empty chair. The teacher said I had to use my voice. I said No, but the teacher kept telling me I had a lovely voice. The strong, mature part of me, the woman part of me, said: 'Do it. Keep going, Liz, keep going.' The child in me was terrified and wanted to stop. My whole life-struggle was happening right there. I asked to sign it first but then something broke in me and I did it in speech. Then I just went right to the chair and cried. When I saw Sue the next day there was an emotional reaction but I understood it. The child had been defeated.

During the early part of the therapy Bob McMahon decided that he had had enough of Chicago and returned to Florida.

Elizabeth was content to go through the painful process of the therapy on her own and found the strength to stay on in Chicago without him. Her work was blossoming and her activities expanding. She was asked to direct an American Bicentennial play for a high school and she had another job teaching theatre to deaf adults.

Feeling more confident, Elizabeth decided to go on an unaccompanied holiday to a distant place where she knew absolutely no one. She chose St Croix in the Virgin Islands and set off with a curious purpose in mind. In the Chicago *Tribune* she had read of a fisherman from the Virgin Islands who had lived briefly in Chicago then decided that the cold climate and the tax man made Big Windy too uncomfortable for him and had returned to St Croix. Many a colourful story was told of Amando the Shark Man, including the occasion when he had fallen out of a small rowing boat while trying to land a harpooned shark and hours later had swum back to the shore pulling the dead shark behind him on a rope gripped between his teeth. It should be said this was the time when *Jaws* was playing in every cinema. Nevertheless, Elizabeth's curiosity (and no doubt also her passion for Hemingway) was aroused by this romantic figure — who walked around with a parrot on each shoulder (one spoke French, the other Dutch, while the Shark Man spoke broken English). She found him during her holiday and was impressed by the elderly man with the weather-beaten face and white hair who stood at the water's edge with a pipe in his mouth, looking out to sea. She talked with him for a while and on the day of her departure a new-found friend came to tell her that Amando had asked after Elizabeth, with the message: 'Where is she? Tell her I want to marry her.'

Another message reached Elizabeth while she was in the Virgin Islands, by telephone from Daytona Beach, Florida. It was Bob asking her to stop off at Daytona on her way back to Chicago. After giving the matter some thought, she decided to accept the invitation.

She flew into Florida to find that Bob had landed a small role in the annual Official State Play, an outdoor pageant called

Cross and Sword which depicted the sixteenth-century tale of a Spanish Captain-General conquering Florida and falling in love with an Indian princess. Bob was to be an Indian dancer and he took Elizabeth to rehearsal. After winking at her across a distance, the director of the spectacular piece offered her a role as an Indian maiden. Once she had joined in, her role was switched to the larger part of a gypsy girl, with instructions to get out to the front and ad lib. This she did for six nights at $20 a week.

Elizabeth returned to Chicago, followed soon after by Bob but the relationship continued to fluctuate. Elizabeth continued the therapy sessions with positive results and her work thrived as she directed more plays and pressed on with her teaching. In 1977 in Chicago there was a World Convention of American Sign Language at which it was declared officially that ASL had arrived as a language in its own right: henceforth it would be taught in colleges as an accredited course like any other foreign language and be taught in the classroom to deaf children. It was an important breakthrough and Elizabeth took pride in the fact that she was there at its announcement.

Anita Quinn was planning to visit her daughter in June, 1977, in Chicago. Elizabeth was anxious that her mother might not manage the journey on her own, but without cause:

> Bob and I went to meet my mother at the station. I was worried about how she would manage her luggage because we were not allowed to go on the platform. But then I saw a very lively little person waving at me and pushing her suitcase along on a trolley. She was perfectly all right and she looked wonderful.

For two weeks Elizabeth and her mother divided their time between touring Chicago and Lake Michigan and going together to the sign-language classes that Elizabeth was teaching. Anita Quinn was curious to know why hearing people wanted to learn sign language; when she asked the students, they told her that it was because they wanted to communicate with their deaf children, friends or neighbours. There were also meals

when hearing friends of Elizabeth's would converse in sign so
that Elizabeth could understand what was being said, and this
again was noted by Anita. The visit was a pleasant one for both
mother and daughter as they began to get closer to each other:

> I knew there was still a long way to go and that I had to
> adjust my relationship with her from being that of a child
> to that of a woman, but it was a beginning. Towards the
> end of her stay my mother came to me and said: 'May I
> have lessons from you in sign?' I just stood there and stared
> at her and the tears came. Why didn't she learn years ago.
> Why now?

From Texas, Elizabeth now received an unexpected invitation
to go to Austin in the summer of 1977 to join in the formation of
an organisation called Spectrum which was being established to
provide facilities for the deaf. It was an intriguing prospect but
first she wanted to go back to West Haven to help celebrate
Billy's birthday. The journey involved another long car drive
but this time in a smart Oldsmobile which she was taking to a
client in Philadelphia for a car-rental firm. She pulled on her
father's old railway cap — a cap she still occasionally wears to
this day — to disguise her sex as she drove through the nights
through Illinois, Indiana and Ohio. On the dark empty roads
the few cars travelling the same direction passed and re-passed
each other with a friendly wave and Elizabeth was comforted by
the camaraderie of the highway. Her thoughts drifted to the
benefits she felt from the therapy course and how she could
now come to terms with going back home to see her mother and
Billy and knowing that her father would not be there. She
dropped the rental car off in Philadelphia and continued by
train to New Haven and the family:

> We talked all day and all night for days. It felt good to be
> home. On the last day when Billy was taking me to the
> station I asked if there was time to visit my father's grave. I
> think I half hoped that there would not be time but Billy
> said there was and we drove to the cemetery. I was shaking

but when I saw the grave it was in a beautiful setting right by a strong, beautiful oak tree with Yale Football Stadium beyond. Billy said you could hear the football players practising. I felt so happy. At last I had really come to terms with the fact that my father was gone.

EIGHT

Spectrum, Texas

The road from Austin to the Spectrum site ran south-west past Oak Hill into increasingly rugged countryside. The suburban sprawl of the city gave way to rolling hills and lush, thickly wooded valleys. This was cowboy country. From Rawhide Terrace, Elizabeth and Bob looked down the rough track they were following to a cluster of buildings with a large white tent alongside: at first they were convinced that they had come to the wrong place.

Elizabeth's surprising invitation to join the Spectrum conference had been followed up by literature and photographs explaining the background and purpose of the organisation. It had been the inspiration of Janette Norman, a hearing woman dedicated to advancing the cause of the deaf, who had found a benefactor named Helen Devitt Jones to help realise her dream. From an initial series of art classes for deaf children in Austin, Janette Norman had seen her project expand into a centre providing both encouragement and facilities for deaf artists. In less than three years the centre was ready for considerable development. The formation of Spectrum, Focus on Deaf Artists, had been announced officially at a conference in Austin in March 1977, just four months before Elizabeth's arrival.

The ranch headquarters of Spectrum, thirteen miles outside Austin, had been acquired only the previous year — hence the need for a tent to accommodate the summer conference. The two visitors from Chicago arrived slightly late at the beginning of August to find the conference already underway, attended by deaf arts delegates from most of the states in America: as the discussions were held in very fluent American Sign Language, they followed the proceedings with some difficulty. Elizabeth's working knowledge of ASL had been gleaned from conversations out of class with the pupils of the American School for the Deaf. Since then she had relied mainly on verbal communication with her family, and had used English Sign Lanugage with its alphabet-based signing in her progress through Washington, Waterford and Chicago.

Elizabeth took a little time to re-adjust to the sophistication and condensed vocabulary of ASL, in which nuances are expressed as much with the face and body as with signed words, and one sign concept can convey several English words or even a complete statement. Her predicament was noticed by Charles McKinney, the president of Spectrum and an imposing figure of 6ft 7ins often topped by a ten-gallon hat. He interpreted for her when necessary and made sure that she was able to follow the discussions. There was another actress present, Ella Mae Lentz, who was a committed champion and exponent of ASL and who travelled the country demonstrating and lecturing on the language. She gave her time generously to Elizabeth. Besides working to improve Elizabeth's knowledge of ASL, the two actresses joined forces to present a sketch in the end-of-week variety show. Their sharp imitations of Spectrum instructors and participants gave great amusement to the audience.

The week in Texas had an immediate influence on Elizabeth. Such a wide-ranging assembly of deaf artists, from fields including dance, mime, writing, painting, photography, design and graphics, was quite an eye-opener. She was also impressed with them as individuals, for their energy and enthusiasm. Whether they were deaf or hard of hearing, while their early lives held much in common with her own they seemed to have emerged with stronger and better adjusted personalities. She wanted to know the reasons for this and, with luck, grow to share their convictions. She also detected that, though still in its infant days, Spectrum was an organisation on the move and she wanted to be a part of its growth. Among the activities launched, it seemed to her that theatre might be neglected; it was in that direction, she knew, that she could make her most useful contribution.

Charles McKinney told her that, under the Comprehensive Employment Training Act, grants were becoming available which would enable Spectrum to make a number of new appointments. Within the terms of that Act the only permanent position he could offer her was that of marketing manager. The specification required 'a creative individual with knowledge of product design and distribution.' This did not seem an exact description of the skills Elizabeth had to offer but if that was all that was available she was not going to dismiss it lightly:

> I had absorbed a lot in that week and I realised I wanted to move down and join them. The ranch was a magical place with deer, chipmunks, rabbits and even the occasional rattlesnake. But there was something in the air; a sense that something was about to happen. I felt that Chicago had been a period of incubation and that now I was ready to move on and find out what I was capable of. The most difficult part was to tell Sue Goldstein I had decided to move away. I said to her: 'I don't know if I am doing the right thing but I feel instinctively that this is what I should be doing.'

Back in Chicago, Elizabeth resolved to make the move even before she was confirmed as Spectrum's marketing manager. She had hesitated only briefly over worries of how she would support herself, remembering that she had come to Chicago on exactly the same basis and had managed to survive. With a dance group already established at Spectrum, Bob McMahon was happy to join her in the enterprise and they began arranging to transfer their home to Texas.

Bob went ahead to find a house in Austin, leaving Elizabeth to wind up their affairs and clear out the Chicago apartment. By now an experienced long-distance driver, she intended to take what furniture they needed to Austin by road. Friends helped her to load up a medium-sized truck and she set out on the long journey south, to discover that McMahon had found them a perfect small house with its own tree-filled garden. As they set to work transforming it into a home of their own, Elizabeth's appointment as the new marketing manager of Spectrum was finally ratified. Her duties were to publicise the work of the visual artists and to mount exhibitions. It was new territory for her but she entered into her new job with a will, determined to learn as she went along.

There was still no commitment to a theatre programme at Spectrum and the first impetus in that direction came not from Elizabeth but from the organisation's secretary and treasurer, Clarence Russell, who had directed, designed and acted in deaf theatre productions before joining Spectrum. He had also staged the conference variety show in which Elizabeth and Ella Lentz had starred with such success. Russell had negotiated with the Zachary Scott Theater in Austin for Spectrum to run their own production and he chose as their first show Dorothy Miles's *A Play of Our Own*. The play was an adaptation of Stanley Kramer's 1967 film *Guess Who's Coming to Dinner*, in which Spencer Tracy and Katharine Hepburn play the genteel parents of a daughter who brings Sidney Poitier home as her fiancé. The stage version had substituted for the racial differences between the lovers a deaf/hearing conflict; it had also transplanted the family from East Coast America to nearby Houston. Clarence Russell was to direct and in the autumn of 1977 he held his auditions on a wooden platform built in the grounds of the ranch. Elizabeth attended the audition in the hope that a small role might be available but she soon found herself cast in the leading role of the daughter, Ruth. The Spectrum members continued their work by day but the cast now met to rehearse in the cool of the evening on the outdoor platform. The Texas evenings made this an unusually attractive working environment but Elizabeth had little time to savour its charms:

> It was the first time I had a real, full role to work on, a characterisation to find, and we were going on in front of a paying audience in an actual theater. All my life I had fantasized about the theater and about myself being in it but this was the reality. Clarence Russell was very patient and sensitive with me, but as the first night came nearer

and nearer I just wished that the rehearsals could go on forever.

During the rehearsals Elizabeth came up with an important contribution of her own. Although her role was scripted to be given entirely in sign language, Elizabeth thought that the daughter would communicate more naturally with her hearing boyfriend by speaking verbally. It was only a question of a few lines but Elizabeth volunteered to speak on stage for the first time and the idea was accepted.

Rehearsals moved in due course from the ranch to the theatre and here Elizabeth found that the playing area was a low stage closely surrounded by seats which gave the actor eyeball-to-eyeball contact with the audience. Early arrivals at the first night may well have been distracted by the sight and sound of an apparently demented figure screaming incoherently in a deserted baseball field near by — they would have been even more surprised to learn that it was the leading lady:

> The tension had been building and building. When I was waiting in the wings I just could not stand it any more. My mind was racing with thoughts that I could still back out and say I was sorry, even if the whole thing fell through. I was so nauseous I could not speak. So I went out on to the field and just screamed and yelled until I had got it all out of me. It seemed to work. By screaming and deep-breathing alternately I made myself calm again.

Elizabeth's first scene was Ruth's homecoming, in which she is greeted by a girlfriend played here by Spectrum member, Alyce DeMers. Elizabeth stood in the wings until her cue arrived, with an old brown suitcase in each hand, soaking up energy from the stage lights and drinking in the atmosphere generated by the unseen audience. Walking on for her first scene, she was comforted to find that Alyce DeMers was acting very much as herself in her part rather than assuming an invented characterisation. Elizabeth relaxed into an unexpectedly natural conversation with her which eased her nervousness at being in front of the audience.

When the play was over, Elizabeth was quite simply relieved to have survived the ordeal. However, her spoken lines proved to have been among the highpoints of the evening. The next day's *Austin American-Statesman* newspaper carried a rave review under the emblazoned headline: 'Everyone should see Spectrum's *A Play of Our Own*. Staff journalist Paul Beutel wrote:

The beauty of this little play lies in the simplicity of its story and message, which the cast delivered with the utmost conviction and charm. Nowhere was this more apparent than in the performance of Liz Quinn, appropriately radiant, intelligent and compassionate as the bride-to-be. Although she speaks quite well, Quinn remained silent until Schmitz arrived on the scene and then they communicated by both words and sign. The blending of the two languages was a symbol of love and total acceptance — one of the loveliest aspects of the play.

There may have been harmony on stage but off stage there was nothing but discord between Elizabeth and Bob. The relationship was foundering and Elizabeth decided to move out of their joint household. She found herself a small apartment in an old mansion and moved in with just a bed, a chest of drawers and an assortment of pots and pans. She resisted the thought of going all the way home for Christmas and instead went off to southern Texas, with a new companion who was more interested in travelling the world in search of the best surf than in seeking any form of liaison with Elizabeth — which suited her fine.

When the Christmas holiday was over, Spectrum decided to follow up their success with a second production in the Zachary Scott Theater. Clarence Russell (known familiarly to all by now as CR) ambitiously chose to mount a stage production of Marlene Dietrich's celebrated movie, *The Blue Angel*, and Charles McKinney was recruited to direct it. McKinney chose Elizabeth for the Dietrich role of Lola, a decision which surprised her as much as it dismayed and disappointed some envious members of Spectrum. The part of the mesmerising seductress was one that was coveted by several of the actresses, who felt they were better suited to it than Elizabeth was. Elizabeth's good fortune did not make her universally popular, but that was the least of her concerns at the time:

I was not sure myself that I was right for the part. I did not look anything like Dietrich and my figure was not that good. I really did not know what Charlie had seen in me for it. He showed me an old print of *The Blue Angel* film with captions on it. Dietrich did not strike me as very seductive, as someone who would have men falling over for her. Visually, I did not think she was that exciting to watch. Also, I was being asked to bring out the woman-liness in me, this intangible feeling of sexual allure, and that was something I had never done before.

Elizabeth's first point of reference for such a challenge was brother Billy with his encyclopaedic knowledge of all things show business. In hour-long phone calls he explained the hypnotic enticement of the Dietrich voice and the irresistible come-hither attraction of her personality. There was also a gay telephonist at Spectrum who was infatuated with Marlene, and here was another rich source of knowledge and advice.

McKinney's intention was to convey the moods and tensions of *The Blue Angel* through sign language and body movement, to display the dramatic potential of ASL as a theatrical language. He also hoped to conjure up for the audience the heady world of nightclubs and cabaret, an environment which the deaf rarely encounter. To his regret, and Elizabeth's, his busy schedule as president of Spectrum prevented him from devoting as much time to rehearsals as he would have wanted. Elizabeth spent long hours instead working with the pianist to pick up the rhythm of the songs she would be singing, accompanied by a few dance steps — she could feel the tempo of the music by placing her hands on the piano. By the first night, the production did not run quite as smoothly as the company would have liked but Elizabeth duly climbed into her laced-up corset, frilly knickers, stockings and suspenders (the first of twenty-two costume changes during the show) and set out to seduce the besotted university professor of the play and, in the process, the audience of the Zachary Scott Theater:

I am not sure how successful we were but in playing Lola I was surprised by what I found in myself. The allure, the sexuality I had supressed for so long began to surface — the know-how of how to manipulate a man. It was something I had not known about before and I enjoyed it for that reason. I could feel the audience becoming mesmerized. It was a wonderful feeling.

Paul Beutel, in the next day's *Austin American-Statesman*, was again admiring: 'When Lola (Liz Quinn) begins her upbeat number she swings her hips to set the tempo for the pianist, who then follows her as she presents her song in sign. On the more sombre side, Quinn's version of Dietrich's immortal "Falling in Love Again" is pure visual poetry.' But there was a dissenting voice in another local newspaper, the *Daily Texan*, which criticised the production for overtaxing the limited resources of Spectrum's dramatic arm:

One example is the lead role of Lola, played by Liz Quinn. The original character of Lola is, for most people, inextricably bound to the image of the mesmerisingly sexy Marlene Dietrich interpretation. Quinn, though a magnificent actress, is a little too old to be right for the role and not really a good enough dancer. The fact that she does a more than passable job as Lola speaks more for her personal resourcefulness than her real compatibility with the role. Her greatest strength is in her use of facial expression to draw the audience into her emotional realm. The sexual allure that Dietrich was able to convey with her voice and physical movements Quinn gets across amazingly well with her face.

Paradoxically, it was the latter review which most pleased Elizabeth. She knew that she was not perfect casting for Lola, she knew that she lacked experience for such a complex role, but her successful use of acting technique to cover her deficiencies and project sufficient quality of the character instilled in her a new confidence. At the last performance of *The Blue Angel*, one particular member of the audience was distinctly more impressed by Elizabeth's portrayal of Lola than the critics had been. A graduate student of communications from the University of Texas, Richard Gibbe was to figure largely in Elizabeth's life for the next year. Already Charles McKinney and Clarence Russell were proposing a new project which would keep Elizabeth busy for many months, and Gibbe with her.

Meanwhile, it was not just the working life of Spectrum which was influencing Elizabeth's development. For all its public-spiritedness, Spectrum itself was an enclosed and inward-looking deaf society living in comparative isolation on the ranch. There was an intensity and concentration of deaf awareness which led Elizabeth to take her first steps on the road to deaf radicalism. In this community, she felt less self-conscious, less of an odd-woman-out than usual; she admired the self-confidence of her fellows and began to identify with the deaf culture more fully than ever before:

> I am not sure if radical is the right word but I was beginning to feel an anger towards the hearing world. I felt that I had been deprived of an upbringing that could have made me a fuller, more mature person. I wanted to be like these people round me. I was feeling angry at my family, the school, the teachers and everyone who had given me the propaganda that we had to be more like hearing people because hearing people were better. I was becoming outwardly protective of myself, more sceptical about hearing people, more suspicious and more outspoken. The more I listened to the stories of other deaf people at Spectrum and how they were treated by their hearing counterparts, the more I was horrified. I had had the same experiences, the same condescension, but I did not know how typical that sort of thing was. At Spectrum they were more positive, saying you are deaf and you can do this and you can do that. The culture was so rich. Deaf poetry, deaf literature, deaf theatre, deaf art and a deaf way of speaking to each other. I was discovering all this with an intensity I had not known before. I had been exposed to some of it at different times but I had not been as receptive because of the propaganda I had been given. Spectrum was an enclosed community, it's true, but I am glad it was. It gave me the experience so that later I could find the right balance between deaf and hearing.

One advantage of Elizabeth's new-found capacity for aggression was a greater willingness to go to battle for the causes she believed in. A regular sufferer from her crusading zeal was Yacov Sharir, who directed Spectrum's dance unit. Whenever a new round of grants became available it was Elizabeth who put forward the claims of the theatre group against Sharir's petitions for extra finance for his dance projects:

> I was always fighting with Yacov. I believed so strongly in a theatre for the deaf. Dance is a more visual and musical art form, more for hearing people. In the theatre I thought we could give deaf people something they had been deprived of, something in their own language. I wanted the money for all the people in the theatre — the actors, writers, technicians, stage staff — so that they could learn and develop their own literature.

While campaigning on the general front, Elizabeth had her own personal challenge to contend with. McKinney and Russell had accepted an invitation to stage the 'Beauty and the Beast' folk tale at the Zachary Scott Theater and they wanted Elizabeth to direct it. She had two immediate reservations. The first was that she was insufficiently qualified to mount a full theatrical production; the second that the script was slanted too much towards hearing audiences. McKinney and Russell persuaded her to accept the assignment and Elizabeth set out to adapt the script to ASL. She invented some subtle and ingenious devices to make the play come alive in ASL — including using a dwarf as messenger when Beauty and the Beast were conducting a conversation back-to-back — and gradually found that the whole play was becoming a metaphor for ASL's standing in society. The Beast became a symbol of the repression of ASL and society's refusal to accept this form of communication, while only Beauty was open enough to respond to the Beast and his precious language. Elizabeth also introduced into the cast a number of children from the Texas School of the Deaf, believing that an involvement in the play would make them see the rich potential of theatre in their lives. The children were trained in English rather than American Sign Language, and confusion quickly followed in their wake:

> The first rehearsals with the children were a disaster. They

were running all over the theater playing tag and hide-and-seek. They did not know what rehearsal meant, they had no concentration or discipline and they did not understand what was going on. After a week of this I was in despair. I dismissed all the adult actors and sat the children round me on the floor and told them the story of 'Beauty and the Beast' and acted all their parts in ASL. When I did that their faces just lit up. They were all making the same sign to me, the Y sign, meaning they understood. Then they started explaining it to each other, exchanging ideas and helping one another. It was a very proud moment for me.

With only three weeks' rehearsal, Elizabeth's production of *Beauty and the Beast* made it to the stage and was well received. Richard Gibbe was again in the audience and this time he came forward. He was looking for a practical thesis for his master's degree: his proposal now was to produce and direct a videotape of *Beauty and the Beast*, to be shot in a studio and sold to television with the long-term target of a screening on America's Public Broadcasting Service. It was a bold plan, promising a consider-able breakthrough both for Spectrum and for deaf access to television.

Elizabeth had her doubts. She feared that control of the production would be taken over by the hearing personnel on the TV production team. Eventually a formal meeting was held at the Spectrum ranch, fully attended by all interested parties. It was agreed to go ahead with the production with the provision that Elizabeth be involved in all stages. She was given the title of director of performance within the production team and given leave from Spectrum to work full-time with Gibbe. She found herself commuting regularly to Austin's KLRN-TV Studios as she adapted a new script for the videotape and planned the production. The introduction to television practice and tech-nology was a new departure for Elizabeth, just as the deaf community was a new world for Gibbe; but the collaboration was a good one.

Gibbe recalled the impact on him of Elizabeth's original performance in *The Blue Angel*: 'Deaf theatre was a new, exciting experience for me. They had interpreters speaking the words at the same time but the significance of doing it in ASL with all the extra, expressive motion was obvious. Liz was extraordinary. She was very sensual and very alluring.' He had attended the next production, *Beauty and the Beast*, with considerable curiosity since one of his favourite films was the 1946 Jean Cocteau version of this story. He knew that it was an ambitious project to take the Spectrum production for video-taping but he was prepared to tackle it at the scale it required. A castle two storeys high was built on set, the limited resources available for the production were stretched as far as they could go by begging and borrowing anything that the budget would not stretch to and teams of volunteers came in to help with the building work. Gibbe: 'At times, it had the atmosphere of "Let's do the show right here." '

The serious work of transferring the show to tape was given due priority. Gibbe: 'Liz and I started adapting the script and she came up with a lot of contributions. She was lip-reading and speaking quite clearly and when we got to know each other we did not need an interpreter. I realised that the deaf people at Spectrum would want to have a lot of control and I knew we had to make sure that everyone felt involved. The whole thing was being handled with kid gloves. There were times of tension. The deaf people wanted to be told what was going on but they did not understand the techniques of television. There were blow-ups from time to time; enough to worry me. People would get angry but then they would make up and be hugging each other. I was a nervous wreck most of the time.'

When it came to shooting Elizabeth stayed on the studio floor directing the actors while Gibbe directed the cameras from the control room. Elizabeth's priority, besides supervising the production and the performances, was to ensure that all the signing was caught properly by the cameras and Gibbe was grateful for all her advice: 'I knew that if the production was not perfect for the deaf people then I would not be satisfied.'

It took three months to tape the play and fatigue intensified the existing tensions. Gibbe and Elizabeth could communicate easily enough, but one day he forgot to call the interpreter, forgetting that the actors still needed her to hand. Elizabeth saw the rising panic among her cast and waded into a public row with Gibbe which ended with her shouting at him, to his chagrin, 'How insensitive can anyone be?' When shooting was over there were still ten hours of tape to be condensed and Elizabeth and Gibbe were obliged to spend long hours together supervising the editing.

From this close partnership a more personal relationship began to grow, the initiative coming from Gibbe: 'She was beautiful. Deaf or otherwise, I had the feeling she could be a great actress. She had a sense of humour and I had great admiration and affection for her.' It was not, however, a completely mutual affection at that time:

> I resisted his attentions. I was more concerned about the work and was very single-minded about it. Even though it was over I still felt a loyalty to Bob McMahon and, quite honestly, at that time I did not want anything to do at a personal level with a hearing man.

Elizabeth had by now found a private escape channel at a place called Barton Springs, where she would swim every day in spring-water either before or after work, or both. The exercise was particularly therapeutic in the early evening sunlight, when she could relax in the pool in the knowledge that a good day's work was behind her. Her social life was at a standstill. She declined all invitations to parties and special occasions, preferring to go on her own to films or to the theatre — anywhere where she could watch actors at work. For any trip to the theatre she could usually manage to find a script in advance. Whenever possible she sat in on rehearsals, on one memorable session watching Austin's star actress, Christine Wallis, prepare a one-woman show, *The Belle of Amhurst* (in which she played Emily Dickinson), directed by Jimmy Costello.

Spectrum was by now preparing another production of its own and had selected Gilbert Eastman's *Sign Me Alice*, an adaptation of Shaw's *Pygmalion*. Clarence Russell was directing and wanted Elizabeth to try for the leading role. The pressures of *Beauty and the Beast* had left their mark on her; she turned down his invitation. The auditions for *Alice* were held in the sports complex of the University of Texas Stadium in Austin. Elizabeth was returning from a swim on the day of the auditions when, after second and third thoughts, she decided to look in to see what progress had been made. She went into the stadium and immediately became lost in the network of stairs and corridors, finding herself eventually on the football field. An elderly couple providentially found her there and took her by the arm all the way to the room where the auditions were taking place. The room was full of applicants but Russell insisted that Elizabeth give a scene which, by her own admission, she performed dismally.

Elizabeth put the episode out of her mind until a few days later when a Spectrum colleague congratulated her on winning the role. She went straight to see Russell in his office to confirm this. The meeting was interrupted by a Spectrum colleague who blurted out an apology to Elizabeth, adding to her confusion. The young woman explained that she had wanted the role so badly that she had complained at the casting and a petition was now circulating in protest at the injustice of giving Elizabeth the leading role in three successive productions. There was uproar. Spectrum president Charles McKinney called a meeting and each member took it in turn to justify the petition. It was a painful experience for Elizabeth, reviving all her old fears of being the excluded outsider; but she heard them out. She explained to her critics, who were mainly from the visual arts programme, that she had not wanted the role, that she had turned up at the auditions more by chance than design and that it was the director who had urged her to take the part:

> I said I had tried a lot of different things in my life and I had always tried hard but acting was what I did best. It was on stage that I knew best how to express myself. I said I had never taken their paintbrushes away from them so why were they trying to take the stage away from me — and then I walked out.

She took a reviving swim at Barton Springs, drove around on
her own for a time, then went home where, in quick succession,
Russell telephoned her to persuade her to stay in the production
and Spectrum founder Janette Norman arrived with the same
message. After much thought, she relented.

Rehearsals started under a cloud of smouldering resentment
and the production proved a difficult one. The *Pygmalion* play
had been transposed into the deaf world, with Professor Higgins
advocating the correct and proper English Sign Language
while Eliza (here, Alice) championed the more flexible ASL.
Russell's main problem was how to manoeuvre his large cast on
such a small set. Elizabeth was given a rousing ovation as Alice
and received a steady stream of visitors in her dressing room
after the performance. It was a couple of hours later that she
slipped away to the quietness of the deserted stage. Sitting alone
she was interrupted by one of the Spectrum staff who had built
the set and signed the petition against her casting. He told
her: 'I'm so glad it was you who played on my set. You were so
right for the role.' Paul Beutel of the *Austin American-Statesman*
spilled over with admiration for Elizabeth — 'the extraordin-
arily expressive Liz Quinn is, as usual, above criticism' — but
he complained about the three-hour production and its static
staging. All the same, the pressures were making life uncomfortable for Elizabeth:

> It had all been so damned hard. Spectrum was new and
> exciting and dangerous. Because we were creating some-
> thing new everyone was full of fire and fierce competition.
> I could understand that. But it was still hard when people
> actually appeared to be putting difficulties in my way. It
> was not that I blamed anyone or thought that any one
> individual was responsible. It was just a situation I found
> very hard to contend with.

There was another contentious issue fast approaching. Elizabeth had been at Spectrum for a year and the grant which had
secured her place as marketing manager was no longer
available. Work on *Beauty and the Beast* was still by no means

complete, so she would have to look elsewhere for income. The answer came in an unusual form:

> Ever since I had moved into my own little flat on 6th Street I had become friends with a woman called Cleo who lived in a beautiful big house nearby. Cleo was seventy-eight years old, a real live-wire, wonderfully funny and slightly eccentric. I loved being with her. She drove round everywhere in a big car and had two gazebos in her garden filled with exotic birds. Those birds were like children to her — she was hip but also old-fashioned, if you know what I mean. Almost every night I would tap on her window so she would know it was me, and then go in and talk to her. So when I needed a job, Cleo gave me one. She owned a lot of property that needed painting and renovating and she also had a daughter who lived in a lovely house in the hills, so I became like a part-time maid for the daughter, doing her cleaning, and I also painted the other houses for Cleo.

Beauty and the Beast had now reached the dubbing stage, with hearing actors called in to provide voice-overs for the signing deaf actors. Richard Gibbe remembers Elizabeth being meticulous in coaching the actors to match their voices exactly with the signing and expressions of the actors on the videotape and guiding them on how strong or soft their delivery should be. Despite Elizabeth's reservations, the friendship with Gibbe was growing into something more and the relationship blossomed when he took her to a New Year's Eve party in San Antonio.

The party was attended mainly by people with artistic connections, including some from Los Angeles's film community. It was Elizabeth's first big social occasion and the fact that she was attending a party with hearing people for more or less the first time amazed her escort: 'That just blew my mind. On the drive down Liz told me how nervous she was and it could have been an emotional experience for her. When we got to the party I was concerned that she should not be excluded or made unhappy but I need not have worried. Inevitably, she became the focus of attention and people were fascinated by her. I really felt quite flattered to be seen with her.' The prospect of such a formal gathering had daunted Elizabeth but once inside the house she was more interested in a large room full of cans of film reels than in the people she met. Towards the end of the evening she and Gibbe were sitting together by a fireplace and here Elizabeth conceded that she was attracted to him. They would have their occasional rows but the relationship was now mutual, and growing stronger.

Between her work on *Beauty and the Beast*, her attempts to set up a permanent theatre department at Spectrum, and her money-raising domestic labours, Elizabeth's time was fully booked when, in February 1979, Clarence Russell approached her with the idea of doing a one-act two-character play by A.R. Gurney. Called *The Golden Fleece*, it featured a husband and wife who chose to play out their marital problems by assuming the characters of Jason and Medea from ancient Greek mythology. Elizabeth doubted that the intricate script would be understood by the deaf simply through signing but Russell firmly reminded her of the scope of ASL as a means of expression and warned her not to underestimate deaf people's intelligence. It was a timely reminder for Elizabeth and one which brought her up short in her deaf radical tracks. She agreed to join the production and played opposite Charles McKinney. The reviews were good but few people saw it in Austin because the show was inadequately publicised.

Nonetheless, *The Golden Fleece* proved to have considerable staying power. The company was invited to perform in Houston and Russell started looking for another one-act play to make a double bill. He chose Chekhov's *The Proposal*, suggesting that Elizabeth should play the daughter. This was the piece which Elizabeth had attempted to play in 1974 at the National Theater of the Deaf, immobilised by nerves and hiding behind her hair. This time she produced a characterisation which allowed the comedy of the piece to emerge much to the audience's delight and her own. From Houston the double bill went on to Kentucky and there were further dates to come.

During the run of *The Golden Fleece* there was an influential visitor to Austin: Tony Barr, the executive producer in charge of dramatic programming at CBS-TV and a co-founder of the Los Angeles Film Actors Workshop. On arrival he held an intensive two-day workshop at the Austin Actors Clearinghouse and every actor in Texas knew that it was an opportunity to move quickly on to greater things. The workshop was for hearing actors and the exercises on the workshop programme dictated that each actor take a partner. Elizabeth linked up with Bob McMahon to attend the sessions and was singled out for praise. She invited Barr to attend a performance of *The Golden Fleece* where he pronounced himself impressed by the production and the performances. There was some interest in Elizabeth also from the local KLRN-TV station, which introduced a new series for children entitled 'Khan-Du'. For one episode, written around herself, she contributed on both the script and the shooting.

On one occasion during the month run of *The Golden Fleece* and *The Proposal*, Clarence Russell went out to dinner with Elizabeth and the conversation took a turn of some significance. Russell recalls: 'The subject of Liz being an actress and her wish of developing into a professional came up. I told her to go to Los Angeles or New York City and try to gain more experience in the field of acting. She became very scared at the idea of the risks involved and of being away from her comfortable and sure atmosphere at Spectrum. I told her that it was time for her to go away. I couldn't "baby" her all my life. If she wanted to be a professional actress, she would not find it in Austin, Texas.' Much later Russell was able to reflect: 'Believe it or not, Liz was the only major accomplishment to come out of Spectrum. In my book, she is the greatest actress. She is one of the very few who can act from the soul, physically and mentally. She is so convincing, well-coordinated and real.'

In September 1979, the three leaders of Spectrum, Janette Norman, Charles McKinney and Clarence Russell, received a formal invitation to attend the first night of a new play at the Mark Taper Forum in Los Angeles. They knew that the play had something to do with deafness but showed little interest in making the trip to California until they mentioned it to

Elizabeth. The invitation was accompanied by a handbill giving only an outline of the play and the leading members of the cast. She read that the play concerned a speech therapist who fell in love with a deaf student. She also read that the leading actress was Phyllis Frelich, the deaf actress whose reputation had long been known to Elizabeth and whose work she was anxious to see. Playing opposite her was an actor named John Rubinstein whom she had seen and admired in Bob Fosse's stage musical, *Pippin*. Elizabeth's enthusiasm fired the others and so the four of them flew off to Los Angeles to attend the opening night. The play was *Children of a Lesser God*.

NINE

Los Angeles

In 1977, unknown to Elizabeth as she joined that first Spectrum summer conference, the playwright Mark Medoff (best known at that time for his off-Broadway hit, *When You Comin' Back, Red Ryder?*) had visited the Rhode Island home of his friend Bob Steinberg and his wife — otherwise known as Phyllis Frelich, a founder member and outstanding actress of the National Theater of the Deaf until she left to raise a family. Medoff had ended that visit with the promise to write a play for them. The playwright had been inspired towards new work previously through various conversations with actors and the Steinbergs touched a nerve in him. He had taken to heart their criticism that there were no roles for deaf actors in the canon of hearing theatre and their own vitality and strength of character had made him all the more determined.

Two years passed during which Medoff became chairman of the drama department of New Mexico State University at Las Cruces. The appointment enabled him to bring in visiting professionals to work with the theatre students and the first people he turned to were Bob Steinberg and Phyllis Frelich. For five months they worked on a script which was not biographical but which drew on the experiences of Steinberg and Frelich as a hearing man and a deaf woman sharing a relationship. The couple took the two lead roles in four performances of the play, now in a stage-worthy form and with the title, *Children of a Lesser God*. These four shows at Las Cruces convinced both participants and spectators that the play had a future beyond the university drama department; the script was sent to six leading theatres across America. Some expressed long-term interest but the most positive news arrived from Los Angeles.

Over thirteen years and some seventy productions as artistic director of the Mark Taper Forum in Los Angeles, Gordon Davidson had established an unrivalled reputation on the West Coast for presenting new and challenging work to a large and popular audience at his theatre within the imposing Los Angeles Music Center complex in downtown LA. Conveniently the Mark Taper Forum still had a slot to fill in next season's schedule: Davidson wanted to see Medoff at his Santa Monica home as soon as possible.

Davidson accepted the play for an October opening in his open-stage auditorium. Director and author had just three months to prepare the play for its professional premiere and major changes were made. The least comfortable change to be made was to ask Bob Steinberg to step down in favour of a new actor for the leading role of the speech therapist, James Leeds. His replacement was John Rubinstein, actor son of the celebrated pianist Artur Rubinstein. Four characters from the first Las Cruces version were dropped and a new second act had to be written. By the time Elizabeth and her Spectrum companions flew to Los Angeles the word was already out that something exceptional was about to happen at the Mark Taper. Expectation was running high.

Elizabeth, Janette Norman, McKinney and Russell arrived in Los Angeles on the day of the first night. They separated to stay with various friends then got together in a borrowed car to go to the theatre. It was Elizabeth's first visit to Los Angeles but her eager anticipation of the play superceded any thoughts she might otherwise have entertained that this was the city which had been so central to the many shared fantasies with Billy:

We got to the theater and it was a glittering occasion. There was a sense of excitement in the air. Because it was known that this was an unusual production people had come from Washington, Chicago and all over. I recognized some from Gallaudet. After Spectrum and Austin, it all felt very big time. It made me feel a bit unsettled but I could not wait to see the play.

A synopsis had been provided for the audience which helped Elizabeth to keep abreast of the swift scene changes in Davidson's fluent production, which was played with minimal scenery and props. From the moment the lights came on out of darkness to illuminate Phyllis Frelich and John Rubinstein on stage, Elizabeth was held spellbound by the two performers and little of the content of the play made any impression on her that evening:

> I was just struck by the relationship of Phyllis and John as actors and what they were doing together. There was such a rapport between them, so much giving and taking. I had never seen anything like this — a deaf actor communicating with a hearing actor at such a professional level. Phyllis was so quick, she was picking up every cue and being right there every time. With so many scene changes on the one set I found the subject of the play confusing and difficult to follow at times. I was just enthralled with the technique of the acting.

But when Phyllis Frelich came to make her main speech of the play, Elizabeth was profoundly affected. The speech is a monologue which the character of Sarah Norman is to deliver to the Equal Employment Opportunity Commission, to win democratic rights for the students at the college for the deaf which she attends. Inundated with advice from a radical student, an uncomprehending lawyer and a husband seeking to be supportive, she chooses to state her own case:

My name is Sarah Norman Leeds, a name I wrote with my fingers faster than you can say it with your mouth. So I will not be keeping you any longer than I would if I were speaking or if, as always is the way, somebody else were speaking for me. For all my life I have been the creation of other people. The first thing I was ever able to understand was that everyone was supposed to hear but I couldn't and that was bad. Then they told me everyone was supposed to be smart but I was dumb. Then they said, oh no, I wasn't permanently dumb, only temporarily, but to be smart I had to become an imitation of the people who had from birth everything a person has to have to be good: ears that hear, mouth that speaks, eyes that read, brain that understands. Well, my brain understands a lot; and my eyes are my ears;

and my hands are my voice; and my language, my speech, my ability to communicate is as great as yours. Greater, maybe, because I can communicate to you in one image an idea more complex than you can speak to each other in fifty words. For example, the sign 'connect', a simple sign — but it means so much more when it is moved between us like this. Now it means to be joined in a shared relationship, to be individual yet as one. A whole concept just like that. Well, I want to be joined to other people, but for all my life people have spoken for me. SHE says; SHE means; SHE wants. As if there were no I. As if there were no-one in here who COULD understand. Until you let me be an individual, an I, just as you are, you will never truly be able to come inside my silence and know me. And until you can do that, I will never let myself know you. Until that time, we cannot be joined. We cannot share a relationship.

No words Elizabeth had ever encountered spoke to her as directly as that speech:

It was about being an individual whether you are deaf or not, about being a person in your own right but with a different language. Phyllis was facing us when she said it and she was very clear with the message. The backdrop was a kind of blue and it seemed to create a glow around her. She used such power to convey that speech and I was thinking: 'Yes, that's what I feel. Yes, I understand exactly what you are saying.'

Elizabeth and the group from Spectrum were among the first to their feet at the end of the performance to join the standing ovation. When they sat down again Clarence Russell turned to Elizabeth and, to her astonishment, said 'You could do that.' The four were invited to the first night party so they crossed the concourse to the Dorothy Chandler Pavilion, the glossiest theatre house in Los Angeles which every year plays host to the Academy Awards presentation ceremony. Beneath the chandeliers, champagne was flowing, long tables were laden with food and the guests were resplendent in elegant gowns and tuxedos. To Elizabeth it resembled nothing so much as a scene from some epic Roman movie; she had never before attended such a lavish occasion. Her own ensemble was a silk dress over which she wore the velvet, patterned, theatre-going coat of old which had been her regular choice for solo expeditions to the much less grand Long Wharf Theater in New Haven.

She particularly wanted to meet Phyllis Frelich to congratulate her on her performance and tell her what an eye-opening experience it had been. She saw the actress across the room, wearing jeans and a headscarf amidst all the finery, and made her way over to her. To her disappointment, she managed only a fleeting conversation. Among the crowd was Freda Norman, Elizabeth's admired friend from National Theater of the Deaf, who was understudy to Phyllis Frelich for this production but about to leave because she was expecting a baby. She told Elizabeth that she had recommended her as a replacement understudy but as she was understood to be fully occupied in Texas the opportunity had passed. She did, however, make a point of introducing Elizabeth to the director Gordon Davidson, who asked her to send him her resumé and photograph. There was another director whom Freda Norman wanted Elizabeth to meet and this director was already looking out for her.

A week earlier Elizabeth had received a phone call from Los Angeles asking if she would play Helen of Troy in an ambitious version of *Trojan Women* using both deaf and hearing actors. The director of the production was a bundle of energy named Rena Down. When she discovered that Elizabeth was going to the opening night of *Children of a Lesser God*, she arranged to meet her at the party after the show. Miss Down had originally considered Phyllis Frelich for her own production until the actress was committed to *Children*. She had then sought out Freda Norman, who was obliged to decline but was at least able to introduce her to Elizabeth. The director had heard of Elizabeth's work and had been told that she was a beauty but might lack experience. She wanted Elizabeth to audition and a date was set for the following Saturday. Elizabeth met others during the party and to her surprise it seemed that everyone she talked to had heard of her. She could only put it down to Freda Norman's generous mentions of her around the Los Angeles fraternity.

Packing as much as possible into her short visit to Los

Angeles, Elizabeth had an important appointment booked for the next day. She had arranged to go to the offices of a top television producer, Norman Lear, who had a network hit with his 'All in the Family' series. She wanted his help to gain a screening for *Beauty and the Beast*. Janette Norman agreed to accompany her on the understanding that Elizabeth would do the talking and the two set off armed with a demonstration tape of 'Beauty'. Norman Lear was out of town but his assistant Frances McConnell saw the tape and discussed its potential with Elizabeth. She was encouraging, saying that she would recommend it to the attention of Mr Lear. Throughout, Elizabeth had handled the sales pitch on her own:

> I was nervous going in. I had gone over in my mind what I was going to say but it came out differently. Leaving that office I thought I had done a good job. Janette Norman said she was impressed with what I had said. I walked out of the building feeling very positive.

Next, Elizabeth took a taxi to the CBS Studios to meet Tony Barr, the producer who had spotted her at his two-day workshop in Austin. He gave her a guided tour of the studio including the control rooms and laboratories, explaining the technology as he went. As she left, Barr recommended that she visit a friend of his in the television section of Twentieth Century Fox. She promptly did so, and was welcomed in a friendly fashion but given the sobering advice that if she wanted to have a career in Los Angeles then she was going to have to live there.

That evening Elizabeth returned to the Mark Taper and paid her $13.50 to see *Children of a Lesser God* again — as she did every remaining night of her stay in Los Angeles. Her friends were off to parties each evening but Elizabeth was hooked on the play and its performers. Before going to the play she would note the address of that night's party, drive there after the performance and arrive so emotionally exhausted from the experience of *Children* that she collapsed on the nearest bed to sleep until she was woken to be told that it was time to return home.

With each successive viewing, elements of the play were hitting home to her as though it were holding up a mirror to fragments of her own life. The relationship between hearing James Leeds and deaf Sarah Norman recalled her own relationship with Richard Gibbe but even more so with Dave Miller, the Connecticut boy who had called at her home after meeting her on a train. Other characters, such as the radical student Orin and the clinging Lydia, she felt she had met before in schools and colleges along the way:

> Dave Miller had taken me to an Italian restaurant, just like the scene in the play, and I had not been sure how to behave. I felt like a little girl with this hearing man. There was the same sense of pursuing and that he was looking after me. I already felt very strongly about James Leeds being too dominant with Sarah, thinking he knows it all. The radical message I understood but did not agree with quite so much. I was still watching the actors. It was the best thing I could have done, better than going to a drama school and trying to learn in a classroom atmosphere.

The day came for the audition for *Trojan Women*. Elizabeth set off for the Los Angeles Actors Theater on Santa Monica Boulevard. In the small, 99-seat theatre she gave a monologue from *The Golden Fleece* then went to talk to Rena Down who said immediately that the part was hers. The director explained how the production would work with deaf and hearing actors doubling in the principal roles, backed up by a chorus of twenty-five. The hearing actors were to have a two-month education in sign language so that they could synchronise with the deaf actors and the complex show would also have a long rehearsal period. As the two women talked the seeds of an enduring friendship were being sown.

On their last day in Los Angeles, the Spectrum group paid a last visit to the Mark Taper Forum and met Kenneth Brecher, Gordon Davidson's associate director, who asked Elizabeth to do an audition for him just as an investment for the future in case there was a touring version of *Children*. He added that Davidson had requested that she be seen before she left LA. In

an empty rehearsal room Elizabeth again gave the monologue
from *The Golden Fleece*, to Brecher's approval:

> It seemed things were happening very fast for me and
> people seemed to be interested. I had got the job in *Trojan
> Women*, I had auditioned and I had met a lot of new
> people. Now I was getting on a more professional level. All
> the plays at Spectrum were on a voluntary basis while I
> worked as marketing manager during the day. I was going
> to be paid for *Trojan Women* and working in front of a
> Los Angeles audience. It was quite a prospect. Clarence
> Russell had seen all this and he knew it was the beginning
> of my flying away from Spectrum. I was beginning to
> sprout wings.

Elizabeth returned to Austin to complete the work on *Beauty and
the Beast*. She and Richard Gibbe showed the tape to an
audience of children at the Texas School for the Deaf and to
their delight the children responded to it with understanding
and enthusiasm. KLRN-TV booked it for a screening later in
the winter. But Gibbe could see that Elizabeth's future lay in
Los Angeles and beyond. They began to drift apart. He went on
to gain his master's degree and pursue his own career in
television advertising.

Elizabeth returned to West Haven for Thanksgiving — her
first visit home in over three years. No sooner was Thanksgiving
over than the Quinns provided her with an early Christmas
celebration, complete with a tree from Bloomingdale's and
presents neatly arranged beneath it, before seeing her off to Los
Angeles. Elizabeth had time in West Haven to prepare herself
for *Trojan Women*. Billy had seen a more recent movie of it with
Vanessa Redgrave, Genevieve Bujold and Irene Papas as
Helen. The old fears began to return as the starting date for
rehearsals drew nearer:

> I felt positive about it, I was looking forward to it, but I
> began getting nervous again and, like with Lola, wonder-
> ing if I was right for the role. I liked Rena. Some of the
> actors were from the National Theater of the Deaf but I

did not know them too well. Once more, I was going to be the new girl on the block. I started having some very strange dreams. One was about Phyllis Frelich being in *Trojan Women* and killing the babies. I think it was a symptom of the apprehension I felt.

There were coast-to-coast telephone calls to Rena Down who advised her on what books she might usefully read for background and Billy had a detailed appreciation of the film version to offer. Elizabeth had brought the script home: with the English text on one side and the ASL translation on the page facing, it helped Elizabeth to understand the poetry of the piece. Then an air ticket arrived from Los Angeles and Elizabeth was on her way to California for her first engagement as a professional actress.

She moved in with a close friend of Rena Down in Los Angeles. Her first call to work was for a meeting with the director and an actress called Rebecca Stanley, who was Elizabeth's speaking counterpart as Helen, to discuss the character. Rebecca Stanley had researched herself thoroughly into the role but Rena Down liked Elizabeth's suggestion that there should be a hint of playfulness in the character as well as the seductive beauty and personality which held men in thrall. The early preparations for the production were conducted in a dingy rehearsal room before the company moved into the Los Angeles Actors Theater. Once inside the confines of this dark and gloomy theatre they had their first run-through. Elizabeth approached her own contribution with misgivings but she was congratulated at the end of the session and decided that she must be moving in the right direction. Rena Down recalled: 'Liz was inexperienced at first. The thing that showed she had not been round the block theatrically speaking was that she would take criticism personally. I had learned some ASL but Liz could lip-read and she became the link between the deaf and hearing actors. She was always very quick and had a sense of humour. My main problem was moving people round on the small stage so that the signing could be seen all round. I remember one day when it was murder. I shouted for them to stop but, of course, only the hearing actors stopped. I threw my clipboard on the stage and Liz was the only one who laughed. She knew what had happened.'

> During rehearsals Rena encouraged me to move around, to do anything I wanted to do, anything that came to me. I was surprised to be able to walk around the whole stage like that but Rena liked it and wanted to keep it in. It came to me to touch Rebecca Stanley, the speaking Helen, on the face as if she was a mirror image of me. Helen was so narcissistic, so wrapped up in herself, so we did that. When the play opened I found that I felt more sure of those moves than I had during rehearsals. They felt right and I could sense that the audience was fascinated by the character of Helen. I was beginning to understand more of the feeling of being committed to a character and having the audience and the other actors on stage responding to that character. There was one scene where I was on one side of the stage and the deaf actress playing Hecuba was on an elevated piece of scenery on the other side. At one moment in the scene I had to swing my arm around and point at her. That gesture turned out to be really powerful. There was a lot of electricity in that one moment. As I pointed my finger at her, her eyes widened, her face was ashen and she seemed to shrink.

Elizabeth had asked her mother and Billy to the first night. They had not seen any of her work at Spectrum so they arrived three days before opening and the family was together again for meals in the evening while rehearsals went on by day. Elizabeth liked the intimacy of the small auditorium and backstage there was one large communal dressing room which helped to provide a good company atmosphere. When the first night arrived the audience was scattered with familiar Los Angeles faces — including Gordon Davidson's — as well as Anita Quinn and Billy. Helen's first appearance was some way into the play. While waiting for their entrance, Elizabeth and Rebecca Stanley stood in the wings with Miss Stanley explaining what was happening on stage. As they waited, Elizabeth's confidence began to seep away. For her entrance, Elizabeth was pushed on

above Charles McKinney
with Elizabeth, rehearsing
The Golden Fleece, 1980.
right Elizabeth
understudying Phyllis
Frelich in *Children of a
Lesser God*, Longacre
Theater, Broadway, 1980
(© Martha Swope)

Elizabeth with Trevor Eve and Gordon Davidson, rehearsing *Children of a Lesser God*, Mermaid Theatre, London 1981 (© Nobby Clark)

Albery Theatre
billboards, London
1981

above Elizabeth and Trevor
Eve, Society of West End
Theatre Awards, London, 1981
(© *The Standard*). *left* speaking
with MP Jack Ashley at the
House of Commons, 1983.
below with Barry Norman,
Society of West End Theatre
Awards, London 1982
(© David Willis)

to the stage by the chorus and thrown on to the floor. She lay face down not knowing quite what was going to happen next:

> When I came up the lights and the sense of the audience were there and the energy began to come to me. I had not been sure if I had the right motivation but I liked what I had created for Helen. It felt good and I could feel the audience being with me. I felt that I was holding the stage. It was a sensation of being in command and very powerful. I liked that — to know that I could be strong was good after the years of insecurity and anxieties.

Billy and Anita Quinn eavesdropped on their neighbours in the audience and reported back to Elizabeth all the favourable comments they had heard. Billy remembered: 'It was really exciting. It was a regular LA theater audience and they were all as impressed with her as we were. She was beautiful as Helen. She played a beautiful bitch and she was very sexy.' There was a glamorous first-night party after the show at the home of Kirk Douglas' ex-wife, Diana Douglas, who had been the speaking actress in the role of Hecuba. The Quinns found themselves being entertained in the heart of Hollywood.

The critics were divided over *Trojan Women*. The *Los Angeles Times* found the exercise too esoteric and others had complaints about some of the acting but Elizabeth emerged with the most favourable notices of any of them. Rena Down had thought the most successful aspect of her production was the twinning of the two girls as Helen: 'Because of the nature of Helen their scene worked best. They were both beautiful but different physically. Helen is self-absorbed and we had the two actresses locked in very closely, touching each other's faces, wrapping their arms round each other. It was very effective. At the end Helen is carried off by Menelaus. I had Rebecca carried but left Liz on stage. Liz stood there letting everyone know no-one was going to get the better of this Helen. She had a smile all over her which said she was going to prevail. She was terrific.'

Trojan Women played three shows a week for a month, which left Elizabeth with considerable time to herself. Her family

returned to Connecticut and she made friends within the
company, making up for her lack of a car in such a sprawling
city. She quickly tired of the city but there were regular forays to
the beaches of Santa Monica and Malibu, interspersed with
days of doing very little at all. It was on one such day, as she was
sleeping, that she received a phone call inviting her to audition
at the Twentieth Century Fox TV studios: a Fox executive had
seen *Trojan Women* and been impressed by Elizabeth's performance. The job in prospect was to join an episode of a
medical series called 'Trapper John, MD'. The audition was
that very day. She threw on a dress, got a set of directions to the
studio, borrowed a car and set off more intrigued by what she
might find than determined to land the role which would
provide her television debut:

> I found the studio and was very pleased that I had
> managed to get myself there. There was a huge poster
> advertising *The Rose* with Bette Midler. I drove through
> the gates to the parking lot where all the stars and the
> executives had their names on the parking spaces. It was
> all very impressive. I found the right office and met the
> casting people and the director. Most of the other people
> there had prepared pieces ready for the audition. I was
> given a script and did a scene with an actor where we were
> man and wife. I was not nervous. I had not had time to
> worry. I was just curious to see what went on and to my
> surprise they told me I had the part.

Several days later she was called to film her segment in the
programme. Her role as a patient's deaf wife occupied only a
couple of minutes of screen time and was shot in one day.
Elizabeth arrived to be sent to the wardrobe department but the
director telephoned ahead to say that he preferred her in the
mauve dress she was already wearing. Inside the lofty, hangar-
like studio she was given her introduction to the techniques of
television acting:

> It was a tiny part but I was excited to be involved in
> television. After working in theater, I was a bit disorien-
> tated at first. The moves were fixed by putting marks on

the floor and it was all very stop-go. I just thought: 'So this is how they do it. This is what it is all about.'

'Trapper John, MD' was a popular series screened across America. When Elizabeth's episode was scheduled a few weeks later, excited audiences clustered around the television sets in West Haven, Port Jervis and other households of the Quinn family. For the celebrity-conscious Americans there is nothing like an appearance on television to confirm a person's existence and identity and her appearance, however fleeting, in a popular TV series raised Elizabeth's career to a new status — at least in the eyes of her family.

With a theatre run and a television performance to her credit Elizabeth stayed on briefly in Los Angeles before returning to Austin, where she was stunned to find the Spectrum organis- ation in crisis. The strong personalities and fiercely competitive spirits within the group were pulling in different directions and not even the founder Janette Norman could control the rifts threatening her cherished community. Yacov Sharir was endeavouring to separate his dance unit from the main body of Spectrum; Charles McKinney had been fired as president and was leaving for New York to set up a deaf theatre company of his own; and Clarence Russell was off to Houston to set up another Spectrum-style project. Elizabeth could see that the organ- isation which had been her base for three years was dissolving. She occupied herself mainly with restoring visits to Barton Springs, from which she was pleasantly diverted before long by an invitation to San Francisco.

The call came from Jane Norman, sister of Freda Norman, who was working on a children's television programme for both deaf and hearing audiences called 'Rainbow's End'. She was planning a writers' workshop to develop ideas for future programmes and asked Elizabeth to join the group. Elizabeth flew to San Francisco in April 1980 to find that the group included Freda Norman, Patrick Graybill (who had admitted her to her first summer course at the National Theater of the Deaf) and other familiar faces from the NTD as well as professional television writers:

Although I knew them they had all been working together over the years, some of them had even worked with directors like Peter Brook and Joe Layton and once again I felt like the odd piece in the jigsaw which does not fit. I was all right at contributing ideas but they were also doing improvisations. They knew each other well, knew their own strengths and weaknesses and could work off each other but I was the Outsider.

Elizabeth spent four uncomfortable days with the group resuming her old habit of taking solitary walks when the others went out to lunch together. When they were each called on to recount incidents from their past the rest of the group came up with amusing and elaborate anecdotes while Elizabeth told them of her father's gift for story-telling and how he had aroused her interest in books. Jane Norman even took her aside at one point and told her that she was interrupting discussions rather than assisting them. It seemed to Elizabeth that she was back in the old NTD pattern of saying the wrong thing at the wrong time. There was comfort, however, on the last day when she ran them the tape of *Beauty and the Beast* to unanimous approval and disbelief that it had been her first involvement in working for television. One of the hearing writers told her privately that he had been touched by her account of her father's influence and that she had a gift, whether she used it in writing or on stage, which she must continue to develop. The workshop ended with words of encouragement for her and Elizabeth took pride in the fact that she had survived another ordeal with some credit.

She left San Francisco with yet another new destination waiting. Charles McKinney had called from New York to say that he wanted her to join him, so she packed her bags and headed east to take on the Big Apple.

TEN

New York

New York theatre falls into three neat categories. First there is Broadway, familiar throughout the world for its bright lights, big stars and glossy musicals; here New York's forty or so main theatres congregate around the famous street as it crosses Times Square. Then there is off-Broadway, which covers the established and independently owned theatres throughout Manhattan; here most of the new plays find their first performance. Finally there is off-off-Broadway, embracing the less formal range of theatrical activity which takes place in any converted church or convenient hall which can pass muster as a theatre. Elizabeth's debut on the New York stage was given in the third category.

After the disintegration of Spectrum, Charles McKinney had moved to New York to create the New York Deaf Theater. He chose for one of his earliest productions a revival of *The Golden Fleece*, inviting Elizabeth to join him for a month-long run. The theatre he found was the Nat Horne Theater at 42nd Street and 10th Avenue—a converted garage where a maximum audience of fifty could be seated on folding chairs. It was only a couple of blocks from the Broadway theatre district but in every other sense it was a good distance from the glamorous big-time theatres. Here Elizabeth resumed her friendship and stage partnership with McKinney as they assumed the characters of Medea and Jason in their dissection of a modern marriage, backed up by a hearing actor and actress who would speak the lines as they signed. Elizabeth moved back home to West Haven and, as the show ran only four performances a week, was prepared to commute to and from the city. *Children of a Lesser God* had transferred from Los Angeles to the Longacre Theater on West 48th Street and from being considered a risk play had established itself as one of the hits of the season. Elizabeth took the opportunity to see it again — another three times.

When *The Golden Fleece* opened its run at the Nat Horne, Elizabeth's speaking counterpart was an actress called Carol Fleming. In the second week of the run Miss Fleming's agent was in the audience, Michael Hartig from the Hartig-Josephson Agency. On a page torn from the programme he wrote his congratulations to Elizabeth on her performance, adding his telephone number and the urgent request that she call him the next day. Elizabeth duly did so and learned that the *Children of a Lesser God* company were looking for a new understudy for Phyllis Frelich and that Hartig wanted to recommend her to the casting agency. Elizabeth was staggered at the suggestion that there was even the slightest possibility of her joining this play which she so ardently admired and she tried hard not to pin any great hopes on such a slender chance. A week later she was at home watching the Tony Awards ceremony, live on television. The Tonys, more properly known as the Antoinette Perry Awards, are the prime awards of New York theatre and there was great celebration in the Quinn household in West Haven when *Children* received the best play award and Phyllis Frelich and John Rubinstein were named as best actress and best actor.

Elizabeth concluded her run of *The Golden Fleece* and within days heard that an audition had been set at the Longacre Theater, where she would be tested for understudy. Her thirty-second birthday was just a few days away and elaborate plans had been made by the family for a day of celebration but the best present of all arrived in the morning mail on 17 July. It was the script of *Children of a Lesser God* with selected passages marked for her to prepare for the audition. Billy had noted that *Children* had opened its Broadway run on his own birthday four months previously. The combination was taken as a healthy augury.

The second surprise of the day came with Billy's announcement that he was engaged to an attractive, dark-eyed woman, Anita Dino, whom he had met at a dance school. He had deliberately held the news until Elizabeth's birthday. The double celebration started with a visit to a marina and lunch, continued with a party at home and finished with an expedition to a roller-skating rink — where, to Elizabeth's astonishment, the floor was suddenly cleared, the lights dimmed and the huge revolving mirror ball illuminated:

> The top instructor came up and took me by the hand and led me onto the rink and we started to dance, just the two of us on this enormous beautiful skating rink. They turned the music up full blast so that I could feel the vibrations and I could see the lights from that huge mirror ball sparkling everywhere. I felt as if the whole world was smiling at me. It was one of the happiest days of my life.

Elizabeth took her first step on to a Broadway stage on 24 July when she went to give her audition in front of Mark Wright, company manager of the *Children* show, at the Longacre Theater:

> I tried to look like Sarah Norman as I had seen Phyllis play her. I curled my hair, borrowed a shirt from Billy that looked like hers and wore jeans. I was so excited just to be there. The theater was empty. I did the scenes with the interpreter from the company and did the speech to the commission.

The interpreter was a girl Elizabeth knew from her earliest days at the National Theater of the Deaf. Jean Worth had been assistant to the NTD director David Hays, indeed it had been her signature on the first letter of refusal when Elizabeth applied to join a NTD summer course. Jean Worth had remembered Elizabeth from those days and had recommended her as the new understudy at the Longacre in the most beguiling terms. She recalled: 'After I left NTD I kept hearing vague things about Liz. When Gordon Davidson and Mark Medoff started thinking of someone for the new understudy I mentioned Liz, but I said she might be too beautiful to play Sarah Norman. That did the trick. They immediately took an interest.'

Jean Worth, who was to become a significant figure in Elizabeth's progress, had involved herself in deaf drama during her college days, subsequently combining this activity with her own career as an actress and, occasionally, as a commercial artist. She still has firm memories of Elizabeth at their first meeting at NTD: 'It was only a brief encounter at NTD but I remember being impressed by how lovely she was. She had a wonderful warmth and bubble about her.'

Elizabeth left the audition with the customary parting shot that the management 'would be in touch with her'. Michael Hartig rang later saying that he had heard that the audition had gone well and calling her into his Madison Avenue office to sign her on as his client. She now had an agent:

> While I was waiting for news Billy and Anita were going on with their wedding plans and I seemed to be on a lonely road again. I went to a reunion of girlfriends from Gallaudet. They had all got married while I was the one who was trying to go on with a career and I felt out of place with them. I began to wonder if it was all worth it.

Out of the blue, *Children of a Lesser God* came towards her suddenly from another direction when Clarence Russell contacted her from Texas to say that the Dallas Theater Center was mounting its own production of *Children*, to be directed by Mark Medoff himself. He suggested that she should try for it. Within twenty-four hours the Dallas theatre called her direct to see if she was interested. Elizabeth remained deliberately noncommital in the hope that if she failed to land the New York understudy job then she would have the Dallas opportunity to fall back on.

Days turned into weeks as she waited for a response to her New York audition and an unwelcome rumour reached her ears. The new understudy was needed because of a proposed national tour of *Children*, in which the New York understudy Linda Bove, whom Elizabeth had known since NTD days, was to play Sarah Norman. The suggestion reached Elizabeth that she was being touted as an understudy for the tour: 'No matter what, I wanted to be Phyllis Frelich's understudy because I admired her so much.'

A much-needed distraction arrived in the form of an invitation to accompany Charles McKinney to teach at an intensive ASL course on a retreat in a New Jersey nunnery. The nunnery turned out to be a beautiful old building set in attractive gardens and she set about teaching social attitudes to ASL to a small group of students with pleasure. All too soon she was called back for a second audition for *Children* and this time the director Gordon Davidson would be there to observe her. She set off for New York from New Jersey by train on a warm August day watching from her carriage the famers at work in the fields and envying the apparent simplicity of their lives. The audition was held in a rehearsal room on the 45th floor of the Minskoff Theater building and she found herself confronted not just by Davidson but by author Mark Medoff and the current stage manager, Mark Wright, as well as a number of actresses who had come from far afield to compete for understudy. She gave her set pieces and was then called over to talk to Davidson:

> He wanted me to come back the next day. I said I couldn't because of the retreat. He gave me another scene to study and told me to come back in an hour. I thought I had done something wrong, that I had gone over the top. When I got back he wanted me to do the scream from the play. I did not know if I could do it or not. I said OK and did it then I just broke down and cried. The room was very still. Gordon came over to me and was very understanding.

Davidson had vague memories of seeing Elizabeth perform in Texas, where he was more impressed with her looks than her talent, but he now saw a real potential in her. He said later: 'When Liz auditioned I felt it was possible for her. Every time we looked for someone to play Sarah we came up against the problem that deaf actresses did not have the level of experience to be able to do it. They were used to communicating with a deaf audience rather than giving an actual performance. But I thought Liz had a chance.'

Elizabeth returned to the New Jersey retreat not knowing the
favourable impression she had made. A social evening was
arranged at the retreat that night but the tension and demands
of the day had taken their toll on her. She had such severe back
pains that she was reduced to lying flat on the floor. The next
day she rang Billy to see if there was any news from the *Children*
company:

> Billy said, 'You got the job.' I said, 'WHAT?' He said,
> 'You got the job.' One of the nuns was taking the call for
> me. I asked her to check again with Billy. 'Are you sure?'
> she said. She was getting so excited about it all that I was
> having trouble lip-reading her.

Billy told Elizabeth that he had spoken again with the casting
director, who had Gordon Davidson standing alongside. The
decision was that Elizabeth was to be the new understudy. She
took her news to Charles McKinney and the students at the
retreat and they all joined in her excitement.

Elizabeth went to Michael Hartig's office to sign a six-month
contract to join the *Children* company. She was to report to the
Longacre Theater in a month's time. She returned to Austin to
close up the apartment she still had there, said goodbye to Cleo
and stored her furniture in a friend's garage, thinking that when
the six months were over she would probably be returning to
Texas. For the rest of the month she worked on the script of
Children with Billy and her mother, who regularly took the part
of James Leeds to her Sarah.

On her first day at the Longacre, the new stage manager,
Jonathan Lee, took her to meet Bob Steinberg, who was John
Rubinstein's understudy as James Leeds, and Phyllis Frelich:

> I was going to be working mainly with Bob. I knew the
> play was partly based on him and that he had been in on
> its development all the way through, so it was very intim-
> idating. I met Phyllis five minutes before the curtain went
> up. She came out of her dressing room in make-up and
> wearing the jeans and red sweater. I was wearing cowboy
> boots from Texas. She said, joking: 'Oh, you are not too

tall.' I guessed I looked all right. I felt they approved of me.

The first work session was spent with Steinberg blocking the moves of the play. Elizabeth was pleased to see one familiar face there — Ken Brecher, Gordon Davidson's associate from Los Angeles, who welcomed her to the company.

After a week she had her first run-through on stage. Elizabeth acquitted herself so well that it was decided to put her on stand-by for Phyllis Frelich immediately instead of four weeks ahead as had been scheduled. Linda Bove, the first understudy who was going to lead the road show, wanted a break so that she could join her husband who was directing a play at the NTD in Waterford. Elizabeth received her first weekly pay cheque of $600 from the Azenberg office and a note congratulating her on being ready to take over so soon:

> They said I was Wonder Woman because I had learned the lines so fast. I was being paid big money but I didn't care much about that. I still had bills to pay off for medical treatment in Chicago and a correspondence course I did in Texas. I wasn't sure if I was ready to go on. I thought: 'My goodness, what will I do if something happens to Phyllis?' Thank God, she always looked so fit and well. Things were moving at speed again. I was a bit unsure but mainly I felt good.

Elizabeth was still commuting from West Haven. She knew the route from Grand Central Station to the theatre but she was beginning to come to terms with life in New York. After the slow pace and cowboy country of Texas and the tranquil calm of the West Haven beach, the high-energy cosmopolitan nature of New York came as a culture shock. Charles McKinney had friends with an empty room in their brownstone walk-up in Greenwich Village and Elizabeth began staying there overnight. The house was full of gay men who made Elizabeth the darling of the crowd, which she enjoyed. She also liked the neighbourhood with its wine bars and antique shops and started looking for her own apartment in the Village.

At the theatre, work was concentrated on understudy

rehearsals with Bob Steinberg, conducted by Jonathan Lee. Both were becoming good friends. She was also watching the play repeatedly in the evening:

> I just could not see myself doing what Phyllis was doing. I felt I was too laid back, too slow. Phyllis had such energy. Even off-stage, her energy was incredible. I thought the safest thing to do was to imitate Phyllis in everything she did. I was a good imitator and I thought that way I would get by. But I began to see there were some points about playing Sarah that I did not agree with. Phyllis, as Sarah, was angry so much of the time that it made it all seem on one level. I thought if Sarah was having a relationship with a hearing man she would not be like that all the time. I thought she would be more vulnerable at times. Also Phyllis was using signed English as well as ASL and I did not think that was right. I saw all this but I was still not sure of my views. But I started to realize that everyone was different and that you could have your own interpretation.

In rehearsal, Jonathan Lee urged Elizabeth to go beyond recreating Phyllis's performance. He told her that what she was doing was good but that she should put more of herself into the part. He took her out to dinner to discuss the character and the play.

While work established itself on a satisfactory footing Elizabeth still had much to learn about other aspects of life in the theatre:

> One day I told Phyllis that I had seen an article about her in the papers. She asked what it was and I said it was about a row she had had with John Rubinstein — they were always having rows. She just got up and walked out. I had said the wrong thing. I had actually said it out of admiration at the strength of a deaf person standing up on her own to a hearing man but she had not understood that. Bob Steinberg took me aside and said that was one thing I had to learn, theater manners. I apologized to Phyllis the next day and she forgot all about it. That's the way she was. There was also the discipline of the theater which was

far more than I had known and which I was not very
good at.

Away from the theatre, Elizabeth's life expanded as she made
the rounds of cinemas and theatres. She saw many shows, from
such Broadway hits as Ian McKellen in *Amadeus* to the current
off-Broadway plays. She also kept in touch with deaf theatre
with McKinney's New York Theater of the Deaf and the
Hughes Memorial Theater which had connections with
Gallaudet College:

> I had always wished that one day I would play there, that I
> could be part of it. When I watched deaf theater I kept
> feeling these were my people. I still did not feel I belonged
> with the *Children* company.

Though she appreciated the encouragement of Jonathan Lee,
she was not always co-operative with him:

> He had a very analytical mind, I knew I was lucky to be
> working with him but I gave him a hard time. I was always
> late and undisciplined. I don't know why but I was. It
> might have been because I was scared, because the pres-
> sure of the job was more than I could handle. It might have
> been a manifestation of being compared with Phyllis,
> especially as I was working with Bob. It just went on and
> there didn't seem anything I could do about it.

When the touring company was formed Elizabeth went to
watch a run-through and found herself sitting next to Phyllis.
She appreciated being in her company and was glad to think
that she would remain her understudy rather than going out
with the touring production. Phyllis Frelich told her that her
husband had said she was doing good work. These were invaluable words of encouragement.

Elizabeth lost Steinberg as a working partner when John
Rubinstein left *Children* and a new actor was brought in to
replace him. David Ackroyd was a New York theatre actor who
had transferred to film and television work on the West Coast.
Elizabeth worked with Ackroyd as he rehearsed himself into the

play. The routine was broken when she had a call from a casting
agent, Phyllis Kasha of BCI Casting, who wanted to see her
about a new television series which was to be given half a dozen
pilot programmes to test its potential as a regular network show.
Elizabeth went to the BCI office twenty-five floors above Times
Square to read for the role with Phyllis Kasha. She was called
back for a full audition with the director James Sheldon and
told on the spot that she had the part. The role was a deaf girl
whose love affair with a deaf boy is jeopardised when the boy's
hearing is restored after an operation. Called 'Nurse', it was
another medical series with a basic hospital setting.

Phyllis Kasha said later: 'We were very concerned about how
the role should be played. Other programmes on similar subjects had not necessarily used deaf actresses. We auditioned
fifteen or twenty actresses who were either deaf or had experience of sign language. We had thought of Phyllis Frelich but
she was not right for the part and she was tied up in *Children*
anyway. Elizabeth was recommended to us both by the
National Theater of the Deaf in Connecticut and by Jonathan
Lee. When Liz first came to my office I knew she was right. The
main problem was getting her out of rehearsals at the theatre.'

A deal was struck that the television company would have a
car on permanent stand-by for Elizabeth in case she was needed
to go on at the theatre and she began work on the hour-long
episode in which she was to be the featured guest star. During
the shooting she made her influence felt beyond creating her
own character:

> The girl I played was a deaf architect but in the script they
> had her writing notes to communicate. An architect would
> have better communication skills than that so they
> changed the script. There were other scenes where they
> changed the dialogue because I thought it was wrong. I
> had problems with an interpreter who kept getting
> between me and the people on the crew. She kept im-
> posing herself. I didn't want to make trouble but Jim
> Sheldon could see there was a problem and fired her. I had
> a friend, Mary Vance, from Texas come in and she would

sign from behind the cameras what people were saying
and no-one knew I was getting interpretation. Billy came
for one day and he did the same. The actor who played my
boyfriend had a very technical approach and did not have
enough feeling to start with. In a love scene he had to kiss
me but it was no good. I told him to really kiss me but there
was only a slight improvement. I did not want the love
scene to be limited. I knew it was for television but I
wanted them to go all the way and end up falling on the
bed or the floor to show that deaf women make love just
like hearing women. I was worried that coming from the
theatre my performance would seem too dramatic and
over the top. Jim Sheldon promised he would tell me if
that happened. He only stopped me once when he said I
was playing to the balcony.

Director James Sheldon was grateful for all the advice Elizabeth
gave him: 'From the start I had wanted a deaf girl to play the
role so that the other actors would relate truthfully to her but
Liz brought so much more to it. She was intuitive about a lot of
things in the script, she was quick and she had a good technique.
She was always concerned about what deaf people would think
of the programme — a concern I shared — and she made sure
that all the signing got on camera. I came to respect her
intelligence, she contributed a great deal and it was the sort of
rapport you very rarely get.'

Phyllis Kasha was equally pleased with her protégée: 'On
these television programs they don't spend as much time as on
films. The whole thing has to move pretty quickly. There were
many demands on Liz from many directions but she handled it.
She was nervous when she first arrived but everyone on the set
loved her. She had a real instinct about acting and took
direction wonderfully. The producers and the network were
very pleased we had found someone of Liz's standard and the
program was well received. It got the best audience of the night
in its time slot and helped us towards getting the series we
wanted. On television Liz had a great quality of beauty. She
reminded me of the young Jacqueline Kennedy.'

There was one embarrassing incident during the 'Nurse'

episode, after Sheldon urged Elizabeth to see Michael Cimino's
four-hour movie, *Heaven's Gate*, in a cinema on the Upper East
Side. Rather than ringing Jonathan Lee, Elizabeth rang the
theatre manager at the Longacre to tell him she would be at the
cinema that night, sitting in an aisle seat at the front, should she
be needed:

> It was the last day the film was being shown in its full
> version before it was taken out and re-edited. The cinema
> was full of actors and directors who wanted to see it, they
> were sitting in the aisles. I thought it was a chance for me to
> learn something from seeing the film and I thought I had
> done a very adult thing by going. The next day Jonathan
> Lee was furious with me and told me that theater
> managers were notorious for not passing on messages.
> They had not known where I was. I had not been fooling
> around like going to a disco or something but at the theater
> the next day I was scolded like a little girl.

Before replacing Rubinstein, Ackroyd was given a run-through
on stage for Gordon Davidson to check his performance. Elizabeth realised that this was a rare chance for her to show her
own performance to the director on one of his infrequent visits
from Los Angeles. Billy came for the run-through and sat in the
empty stalls. Largely because they were both trying so hard to
impress, neither Elizabeth nor Ackroyd gave of their absolute
best but Davidson seemed satisfied. Elizabeth brought Billy
from his seat to meet Ackroyd and Davidson and, because she
was in her brother's company, introduced him verbally. It was
the first time that Elizabeth had spoken since she had arrived at
the Longacre and Ackroyd, for one, was amazed to learn that
she could speak. Jean Worth had heard her voice previously
although they normally communicated in sign. She said: 'I kept
telling Liz that she had a beautiful voice and she should use it
but she was so insecure she would not say a word.'

After the run-through Elizabeth and Billy went to eat and
had a long conversation about why she was not using her voice:

> I told him I was scared but he said I should not be scared

and encouraged me to use it. He said if I was going to have a career people would have to relate to me and I should be using my voice; that I was a different person when I spoke. After this very emotional meeting he put me in a taxi, and I looked back to see the most incredible sight. With all the lights of Broadway on, there was Billy, standing alone in the middle of the momentarily empty street, signing, 'I love you'. Just the lone figure of Billy beneath the Coca-Cola sign. I was so grateful to have a brother like that.

Elizabeth found an apartment of her own in Jane Street in Greenwich Village, rented to her by a doctor who was going abroad. He told her he was not supposed to sub-let and if the landlord found her she was to say she was a visiting relative. With the help of some friends she redecorated the apartment, moved in some pieces of her own and so at last had her own home in New York City. She had also opened her own bank account in Manhattan and was using the subway; all in all she was feeling more part of the city.

Shortly before Christmas Elizabeth was told that Phyllis Frelich was to have four days off in January to film a Barney Miller programme for television and that she, Elizabeth, would take over as Sarah for five performances, starting with a Wednesday matinee. It seemed too soon to be going on and she was anxious rather than elated at the opportunity. The Quinn family more than made up her quota of excitement and started planning a mass outing with relatives booking for the show from Port Jervis, Connecticut and elsewhere. Shortly before the date, Ackroyd's mother-in-law died and he returned to California, leaving Bob Steinberg to play opposite Elizabeth.

The day of the first two performances arrived and Elizabeth and Steinberg were concerned that the audience might reject a show in which both the lead characters were played by understudies. He held his nerve and took Elizabeth for an early lunch, telling her to relax, enjoy the performance and have a good time. Back in the dressing room as she was curling her hair for the matinee, the nerves began to gnaw at Elizabeth and she ran into the street to buy some comforting chocolate. She ran straight into her family and her agent Michael Hartig, who wanted to know what the hell she was doing in the street with curlers in her hair.

Elizabeth took up her opening position on the darkened stage before the lights and the curtain went up:

> I could feel a tremble through the stage which I thought must be a subway train going through. In the dark I was glad to be connected with anything that meant life was going on. The lights went up and I could not believe I was actually there on stage. I looked at Bob and I'm sure my eyes were wide with terror. I could see that with his eyes he was trying to tell me it was all right, trying to comfort me. As the scene went on it got better. It was a wonderful feeling under the lights, sort of warm and hazy. Out of the corner of my eye I could see the occasional movement in the audience. It was nice to feel I could communicate with them but I was glad when Act I was over and the intermission arrived. At the interval the rest of the cast said I had done well and when I went to change Jonathan Lee too came and said it was going well.

As she took her place on stage for Act II, Elizabeth saw two figures watching her from the wings. One was Lee and the other was the producer, Manny Azenberg, who earlier that day had sent her twelve bottles of champagne as a good luck present. She had never spoken to him so far. While the audience were taking their seats he walked towards her, nodded and kissed her. Then without saying a word he turned round and left. Had he liked what he had seen? No-one knew:

> In Act II I got hold of the reins and it felt as if I was soaring right through to the end. I felt very strong, very sure and very proud. I was in a daze. I didn't believe I had done it.

For the evening performance, a full turn-out of the Quinn family filled four rows of seats in the theatre, giving Elizabeth a standing ovation of their own before taking her for a celebration dinner at a nearby wine-bar, where they reported all the glowing comments they had heard from the audience around them. While they were there, one of the stage crew came in and set down a bottle of champagne on the Quinns' table: 'I knew then that I was accepted.'

Elizabeth had survived her first day with no mishaps. Nothing went seriously wrong until the second evening performance. Midway through Act I she had a scene in which Sarah is seen about her duties as a college maid and makes her entrance dressed in overalls and pushing a large trolley loaded with cleaning equipment. On the second night she was in the wings waiting for the cue light (red light for Stand By, green light for Go) and talking to a stage hand:

> I turned round and saw the red light was on and just went, pushing the trolley. I got on stage and realised I was there too early. Bob was still in the middle of a scene with Sarah's mother. I was not supposed to be there. I didn't know what to do. I started fumbling with the things on the trolley to kill time and I cut my finger on something. It started bleeding. Bob finished the scene he was doing and started our scene. He must have wondered what was going on. My finger was still bleeding and I had to interrupt my signing to suck it every now and again. We got to the kissing scene on the floor and I felt my ear being tugged. I had caught my earring in Bob's waistcoat. I was struggling to get it free but he thought I was doing some new moves to show the passion of the scene. I was stuck to him by my ear and my finger was still bleeding. The earring was torn out of my ear and I thought it must have torn my ear lobe. I watched him to see if he was looking at my ear and when he didn't I guessed it was OK. The whole scene was chaos. I felt really down about it, that I had really messed it up and thrown away all the emotional impetus. But Bob and Jonathan came and told me it was theatrical tradition that things always went wrong on the second night.

Elizabeth's series of performances passed without similar incident and David Ackroyd returned to join her for her last show of the week. She had survived the ordeal and emerged with many admirers. Within a flow of fan mail came one letter which, to her surprise, was from the producer of a leading TV chat show, saying how good it had been to watch an actress who really knew her craft.

Bob Steinberg retained pleasurable memories of the shows they did together: 'I remember her being very nervous. It was very much a living performance we did together. It was about support. When I was with her on stage she was always willing to make connections, willing to give and take and there are a lot of actors who would not normally do that. I always used to say how alive she was. I remember I used to get so much from her when we played together. She seemed so happy and so grateful. We had a very special relationship. For me, it was a nice change to be allowed to help someone else. I liked that.' Jean Worth was away when Elizabeth first went on, but caught her later performances: 'There was a lack of technique and discipline about her but she was so volatile and open that it more than worked. Liz had tremendous audience appeal. She was so attractive and easy to watch. I told her after she had done it that I thought she was good but I still wanted to see more from her. I thought she was capable of giving more.' Charles McKinney saw her play Sarah and was pleased for her but with friendly honesty told her that 90 per cent of the performance she gave was actually Phyllis's:

> I think I would have been more excited about it if I had been to acting school and had some technique and know-ledge to fall back on. But I was naive. It did not sink in that this was the professional way of life in the theater. It was only later that I understood what a responsibility there had been in doing those shows. They gave me the feeling that maybe I could be good but first I had better learn some of the fundamentals of working in the theater. I was pleased when it was over and I was more than happy to welcome Phyllis back and take my place as understudy again.

Shortly after Elizabeth's spell on stage Jonathan Lee announced that he was leaving the company. It was a disappointment to Elizabeth as not only had he helped her prepare herself for the show, he had also talked to her encouragingly and at length about using her voice more. He was replaced by a tougher breed of stage manager named Frank Marino who ran the show with tighter discipline making the understudies turn up at the theatre every night. He was rather more demanding on Elizabeth during rehearsal:

> Out of loyalty to Jonathan I did not accept Frank at first. We didn't get on. He did not sign and we only talked through Jean Worth interpreting. He was rough on me in rehearsals. We had a confrontation when I asked him why he was always picking on me. He said that I did not give enough, that I was lazy. He said I was an imitation of Phyllis and if that is all I wanted to be then it was fine by him. I thought I was working hard but maybe I was not working the right way.

Frank Marino was a devoted admirer of Phyllis Frelich and he made few concessions in his dealings with the rest of the deaf actors. He said 'I accepted the fact they were deaf but then they had to show me they could act. They had no discipline whatsoever. The old-fashioned discipline you take for granted in the theater just did not exist. They could not even get to work on time and Liz was the worst of all. She was a chronic late-arriver. We had a big fight once when she was supposed to have been at the theater but she went to the movies in Queen's. I made damn sure they were on time at the theater eight shows a week.'

In rehearsal, he was determined to bring the best out of Elizabeth: 'By the time I got there she knew the rôle, she knew how to play it and she knew the signing. But whatever she did I just didn't believe it and I don't think she believed it. She did not have the truth of it. If necessary, I was prepared to kick it into her. She could be like a spoiled child. She demanded respect but I taught her that first she had to earn it. I tried to draw something of herself out of her. She had lousy concentration. A sure way to get it was if I turned my back on her. Boy, she hated that. We worked two or three times a week and for a long time it was a mess. I guess it came down to insecurity. The fear of not being able to do it, of being found out. Maybe I did come on strong but I did not see the deaf as a special case. If they wanted to work in the hearing world they had to cope with it or get the hell out. Tough shit.'

Two months after her first stint on stage Elizabeth was booked for another run of performances but this time it would be for a fortnight while Phyllis Frelich took a holiday. When the time came, Frank Marino came to her aid and supported her through the two weeks with detailed and positive advice on her performance. The Quinn family came in force again and with the longer run Elizabeth had more time to settle herself into the role. The only disturbance came on the home front when the landlord of her Jane Street apartment discovered that his property had been sub-let and told her to leave. Half way through her run she had to move out and begin commuting from West Haven again. She found another room on Columbus Avenue with friends of Jean Worth and even became accustomed to the fact that one of the girls was a Buddhist, given to holding ceremonies involving candles and incense in the middle of the night.

Life was settling into a comfortable and enjoyable pattern for Elizabeth. She was more at ease in the theatre and liked being part of the Broadway scene:

> After the two weeks on stage I was happy to be an understudy again. I got a craze for doing jigsaw puzzles and everyone else in the theater joined in. I began to feel they were friends and I relaxed a bit and became less defensive. There was a good company feeling. I was happy, I felt more part of it and I even got friendlier with Frank Marino. Going home every night I used to walk up Broadway past the bars and the porn parlours and the restless crowd looking for something but not knowing what. I was never afraid. I felt part of them. There was the same sort of restlessness in me. It was all so colourful and alive. I loved it.

Bob Steinberg saw the changes in her: 'Liz developed, but in personal ways as well as professional. She became less rebellious, less angry and began to soften a bit. She was very defensive about being deaf in a hearing world when she arrived but she began to see things more clearly. She became able to deal with individuals as individuals rather than categories.'

The satisfied contentment was soon broken and in the most sensational way. It started when Frank Marino told Elizabeth that Gordon Davidson was in town and wanted to see her at 4.00 p.m. the next day. The only reason she could come up with for such a call was that possibly he wanted to audition her to join the touring company which was already out on the road. She took Charles McKinney to the theatre for company the next day but left him in the alleyway to go inside to see what Davidson wanted:

> I went into the theatre and Gordon hugged me, which made me feel good as I had got the impression he did not like me too much. I thought I was going to be asked to do an audition but the very first thing he said was: 'I would just like to ask you if you would like to go to London?' I didn't understand what he was talking about. Then it began to dawn on me. There had been talk about the show being done in London and everyone thought it was between Phyllis Frelich and Linda Bove to go there. I knew there was an English actor over [in New York] who was learning to sign with Jean Worth. When it clicked, I said I didn't know if I wanted to go. Could I do it? Suppose the English audience did not like me? I said I thought British deaf people were more oral and might not like the sign language. Gordon said that was the risk I would take. I was very happy being the understudy in New York. I thought why spoil it?

The English actor, Trevor Eve, was sitting in the theatre with his wife, Sharon, when Davidson broke the alarming news to Elizabeth. Davidson called him up and he and Elizabeth met for the first time. Elizabeth vaguely recalled Jean Worth saying that Eve was anxious to meet her but she had never understood why. The two of them went on stage and played out a couple of scenes. Jean Worth signed secretly to Elizabeth that she had heard Davidson say he liked the chemistry between them. More than somewhat confused, Elizabeth left the theatre saying that she would have to think about it first and then decide. Instead of returning to her apartment she took the train to West Haven where both Billy and her mother were delighted at the new development and urged her to go.

Unknown to Elizabeth, there had been a great deal of activity taking place around her which amounted almost to a benign conspiracy to get her to London. The British production was to be presented by producer Ray Cooney, working in association with another producer and theatre owner, Ian Albery. The show would open at the Mermaid Theatre then, barring disaster, go on for a West End run. While he was trying to put the London company together, Davidson was already under pressure with a new Neil Simon show which had run into trouble on an out-of-town date at Boston on its way to Broadway. Thoughts of collecting an entirely British company for London had to be put aside when no deaf British actors could be found with sufficient professional expertise to play the roles. Davidson: 'When we began talking about London we thought about Phyllis and Linda but I remembered seeing Liz. Her performance was still a bit unformed but she seemed interesting. I thought she was ready. I thought she was right but I was not absolutely sure. What convinced me was when I saw her and Trevor together. There was potential in that relationship and it was then I knew I was in the right ball park.'

There had been other conversations elsewhere. Manny Azenberg had been struck by what he described as the stunning sensuality of Elizabeth. He said: 'Without being paternalistic, I knew that whoever was going to play that rôle in London was going to have the experience of their lives. I told the director he could go off and see whoever he liked but I knew that the girl going to London was going to be Liz Quinn. In my business you have to deal in enough shit so why not get involved in some joy. We have so many crappy stars around and here was Liz and she was going to be a real Cinderella job. I loved it.'

Phyllis Kasha, who had struck up a friendship with Elizabeth after she had cast her for 'Nurse', had a casual lunch with Marvin Shute, one of Ray Cooney's associates, during which the conversation drifted towards the London production of *Children* and Shute said they were looking at Linda Bove. Miss Kasha: 'I told him he was making a big mistake and that he should look at Liz. I told him about her work on "Nurse". I had seen her go on as Sarah with David Ackroyd and I told him how terrific she had been. This wasn't business as she was not a client of mine or anything.' Jean Worth, through working with Trevor Eve, had learned earlier that Elizabeth was the favourite for the London job and had only just managed to restrain herself from saying anything until Davidson made the official offer.

The dilemma was Elizabeth's and the more she thought about it the less she felt able to make a decision. Without committing herself she began to work with Trevor Eve but only after a series of misunderstandings:

> I liked Trevor. He seemed nice to me and very hard-working. But the stage management had been putting some bad rumours around that he made John Rubinstein look like an angel. There were a lot of misconceptions. Trevor wanted to rehearse but not in the theater. Because I was on stand-by Frank Marino would not let me out of the theater. Trevor wanted to sort all this out so we met in a little room in the theater then started working in his apartment off Madison Avenue.

Jean Worth remembered Elizabeth joining the work sessions where she had already been teaching Eve signing for several weeks: 'It was a time when they were both sizing each other up and being careful. Trevor was still putting in over fifty hours a week to perfect his signing. He was determined to have it perfect by the first rehearsal, and he did.'

At home, Anita Quinn knew that Elizabeth had to make her own decision and she believed in her daughter sufficiently to know that, if she decided to go to London, she would make a success of it. Billy Quinn, who had visited England, was more specifically positive: 'I had been to the theater in London and to the West End and I was convinced Liz would love it. We have a great mystique about English actors and I thought if Liz could go over there and really click it would be quite an achievement. I knew Liz would be OK as an actress, I knew the strength of the play. My only reservation was, would the audience grasp the play and accept it? I don't remember having any reservations on how she would survive in a strange environment. I had every faith in the English and I didn't expect any problems.'

Elizabeth was at home in West Haven when Michael Hartig rang her to say that negotiations with the Cooney office in London had reached a stage where she must say either Yes or No immediately. Billy took the call and in communicating it to Elizabeth gave no display of his own feelings (neither did Anita Quinn):

> I looked at Billy but he did not want to say anything or give any hint. He just looked at me but I could see he was tense. I looked and looked and then I said: 'Yes, I'll go.' We were all pleased and I was pleased because I had made the decision on my own.

Once committed, Elizabeth suddenly had a thousand things to do from signing contracts to getting her first passport and she still had another two weeks as understudy which gave her just three days between leaving the theatre and the date of her departure.

She wanted to finish her sojourn at the Longacre Theater without emotional farewells but between shows on the final Saturday a party was held for her with presents from all the company. Phyllis came over and sat next to her. 'So I'm losing you,' she said. 'You were a good understudy. I'll miss you.' Elizabeth was overwhelmed. She waited for the curtain to go up on the evening show, watched Phyllis from the wings for five minutes then discreetly left. In the alley beside the theatre she met Frank Marino. He told her: 'It took a long time for us to understand each other and now that we do I am losing you.' Marino said later: 'By the time Liz left she was in good shape. It may have been difficult for her but she had learned how to act. She had begun to draw on her own experience instead of just being a very good mimic.' Elizabeth left the theatre, drove to her apartment, filled her car with her belongings and headed for West Haven:

> On that drive I had so many things going through my mind. I was going on to something new again but something so different from anything that had happened to me before. I did not know if I was doing the right thing and more than ever whatever I did I was going to have to do alone. I was very upset that night and had to get up in the middle of the night to be ill.

The next day Anita Quinn told Elizabeth to wear something nice as they were going to Billy's house. Elizabeth could not understand why she had to dress up to go to her brother's home but when she got there she found the whole Reilly family gathered from Port Jervis and beyond for a farewell party. Their presence only added to the stress which was growing within her:

> I felt under tremendous pressure. I wanted them to support me. I did not think they understood what I was going through. I was very rough on my mother. I had to go downtown to buy luggage. There were a million things to do. I did not feel my mother was paying me enough attention. She was too busy looking after the relatives and the family.

The next day the family gathered at Anita Quinn's house for another party and Elizabeth's patience finally snapped. She shouted at them: 'Why is everyone doing this to me?' Then she walked out and slammed the door. Billy could see the turmoil that had gripped his sister. 'For two days before she left, Liz exerted a lot of hostility towards us all and especially towards Mom. After Liz had slammed the door we all went down to the beach. Mom wanted to get there to breathe some salt air and regain her composure. Liz came down to the beach and said she did not want a ride to the airport and that she would do it all by herself.'

On the day of departure the family was again on the beach, where Elizabeth drove to find them:

> It was a beautiful day with a clear blue sky and they were all having a wonderful time. I said I was sorry for what I had done and they all said not to worry. They seemed to understand. Then I asked Billy to give me a lift to the airport.

They drove to their mother's house where Elizabeth gave her a book entitled *The Giving Tree*. Inside it she had written: 'I hope some day I can be as strong and give as much as you have given to me.' Billy witnessed the scene that followed. 'That did it. They collapsed in each other's arms in tears. The volcano, that tidal wave of emotion, was over.'

Elizabeth drove off to Kennedy Airport with Billy and his wife, Anita. They stayed together for as long as possible, until Elizabeth had to go. Billy said: 'The only time I got emotional was when she walked off. We waved until she was out of sight. Then we knew she was alone.'

ELEVEN

London

The Laker Skytrain DC-10 dipped its port wing towards the Manhattan skyline still visible in the gathering dusk and wheeled north to head out over Nova Scotia and Newfoundland for the night flight across the Atlantic. As she loosened her seat belt, Elizabeth took stock of the whirlwind events of recent days and the unknown future which lay beyond touchdown at Gatwick Airport in six hours' time. She thought about her father, of the family she had left behind, of the friends she had made in Texas, of her other family at the Longacre Theater where she had eventually found a rare contentment, and of the work which lay ahead of her in London:

> I was in a very emotional state but I tried to contain it. So many thoughts were racing through my mind. I remembered my mother standing outside the house, crying, as we left, and how she got smaller and smaller as I looked back. I thought of Billy and his wife Anita as we waved goodbye at the airport. I could so easily have turned round and gone back, gone back to laugh and be happy on the beach and just dream about being on the stage. It is much safer to dream than to actually do it. It had taken a lot of guts and courage but I had kept going. I remember thinking my father would have been proud of that. He had always said I could do anything I wanted to. I was hanging on to that thought.
>
> This trip was the most difficult thing I had done since leaving home after my father's death. Now I was on the plane there was no turning back. Wherever I had been before there had always been the chance to go back home if things went wrong but not this time. It seemed that all the time in Chicago, Austin, Los Angeles, New York, and all the other places I'd been, had been a preparation for

this. I remembered that party for me at the Longacre and how safe it had seemed there, even with Frank Marino by the end. I wondered what was waiting for me in London. How would I get on with Trevor Eve? The idea of working with a hearing actor, who, I assumed, was more intelligent than me, was worrying. I was concerned about working with Gordon Davidson. He was always so much on the move, I did not know him very well. The same questions kept coming back. What would become of me? Would I be able to cope?

At this point, she gave herself two or three months at the outside, as the few clothes and books packed into her two cases testified.

Elizabeth has never forgotten her neighbour on that flight. He was on an expedition to Scotland to find a monster, not in Loch Ness but in another loch farther north, and he regaled her with his plans. Much as she wanted to think quietly about her own life, she began to admire his purposeful enthusiasm for such a bizarre project and felt a bond since she too was on an unlikely mission, the results of which were equally unknown. She just wished that she could bring the same cheerful optimism to the task ahead of her.

Elizabeth's first taste of her brave new world was an uncomfortable experience at the Gatwick passport checkpoint. She did not have the immigration papers which would allow her into the country to work rather than as a visitor. Escorted to a small office, she finally found a letter from Ray Cooney Productions and, in sign, tried to persuade the uniformed passport control officers to ring the Cooney office to sort out the confusion. It was to no avail. She was left on her own under the distant but watchful eye of one of the officers and sat there not knowing what was to happen next. It could not have been a more miserable introduction to the country which was to be her new home.

While Elizabeth was trapped in the passport office a car was speeding towards Gatwick. Philipa Ailion, company manager on the London production of *Children*, had the necessary immigration papers with her but was late arriving. Elizabeth had been waiting dejectedly for some thirty minutes by the time Philipa Ailion found her. The necessary papers were exchanged, they collected the luggage and set off for London. Jean Worth had arrived a couple of days earlier and had taught Philipa Ailion just enough sign language to be able to introduce herself and explain who she was. There was little conversation during the drive as Elizabeth mouthed a few words of response to Miss Ailion's amateur signing. The route took them through Brixton, scene of recent race riots which Elizabeth had read of in the New York papers; the damage and devastation there only increased her gloom. It was a grey unsummery July day and when Philipa Ailion pointed out that they were driving through Trafalgar Square Elizabeth could only think how dismal it looked.

The car stopped at an hotel just off Trafalgar Square and Philipa Ailion took Elizabeth through registration to a room where she could rest after the flight. They agreed to meet again a few hours later to introduce Elizabeth to the Cooney office and the hotel room door was left unlocked so that Ailion could get back in to fetch her. At the producer's office, Cooney's production executive Hymie Udwin was waiting to greet her: she was not in the best of humour. Jean Worth was also there: 'The minute I saw Liz I knew there was going to be trouble. Something was terribly wrong. She was tension from head to foot — and she seemed less than gracious. I did not know what was wrong. It was only later that I understood how difficult she had found the separation from her family and her life in America, and how nervous she was about taking over from Phyllis:

When I went to meet Hymie Udwin he seemed to have a hard face. He looked at me and said: 'Now what have you done before?' I felt he was really saying that I was an unknown and they were doing me a favour. I felt that I was being examined and I got very defensive. I was angry because I thought they had been under pressure to bring the show over here and that was the only reason they had taken me. After a while Jean took me in another room and said I must not show my anger, that I had to smile at these people. We went back in and I smiled and smiled. Hymie's wife came in and said: 'Isn't she lovely?' I think it was then that Hymie melted.

Philipa Ailion, who was at the meeting, said: 'It was very difficult. I think men more than women have difficulty communicating with a deaf woman. Hymie found it very hard to talk to Liz. Everyone, apart from Jean, was new to her and she was very uptight and insecure. I was there to smooth things along and make her know she was welcome but I could sense her attitude.' Elizabeth and Jean Worth were taken to dinner by Philipa Ailion that evening. The restaurant was Italian, Elizabeth's favourite, but when the mozzarella turned out to be mere cream cheese it confirmed her growing belief she had made a mistake in coming to London. It seemed that nothing would go right.

The following morning, Elizabeth had her first meeting with the theatrical agent appointed by Michael Hartig's New York office to take care of her affairs during her London stay. Felix de Wolfe paid her the courtesy of calling at her hotel, the first time an agent had actually called on her. After the New York sharpness of Hartig, with his casual dress and long hair, the elegantly suited and very English Mr de Wolfe provided quite a contrast; over coffee and croissants, however, she warmed to her new representative and felt that her interests would be well protected in London.

Philipa Ailion had booked two apartments for Elizabeth and Jean Worth during their stay. One was in Baker Street (with a commissionaire on the door, which was felt to be an advantage for Elizabeth) and the other in St John's Wood. They went to inspect their new homes and Elizabeth took an instant dislike to the Baker Street premises:

It was the sort of place an elderly aunt might have just died in. The furniture was old and the decor was olive green. I resented the fact there was a guard on the door. I didn't want to be protected. I had lived in New York City without a guard and travelled all over. I did not like the producers thinking I could not live on my own.

The St John's Wood apartment was a modern studio and more to Elizabeth's taste. Set on the 7th floor it had just a hint of New York about it and just around the corner in Abbey Road were the recording studios made famous by the Beatles — and the pedestrian crossing on which they were photographed for one of their album covers. She liked that. That evening she had her first taste of London theatre when she was taken to see Tom Conti and Gemma Craven in the Marvin Hamlisch musical, *They're Playing Our Song.*

The Friday of that week was her thirty-third birthday, which she celebrated by moving into her new home. There was a birthday gift of a new blouse from Jean Worth and a bouquet of flowers from the Cooney office. Without unpacking, she took a taxi to collect Jean Worth for an important meeting with Hymie Udwin at the Cooney office, which Trevor Eve would be attending:

> When we walked in I saw bottles of champagne and wine, food and a birthday cake. I was so moved. I had always spent birthdays with family and lots of friends. Trevor arrived and had a present of a book about films for me. Hymie said he was sure I was going to be great in the play and I felt a little better with him.
>
> Jean told him I could speak. She was always telling people about my voice and encouraging me to use it more. Hymie asked me about it and I said I did not speak because I did not feel comfortable but I hoped I would in a while. He liked that. I began thinking perhaps things were not so bad after all.

From the birthday party Elizabeth went for a walk on her own and found herself in Leicester Square amid the showcase cinemas, tourist gift shops, record stores and coffee bars:

> It was like New York, like a small Times Square, with the neon lights and all the activity. I bought a kebab in pitta bread and sat to eat it in the middle of the square. I wasn't

afraid. I loved it. I'm sure there was a lot of noise around from the video machines running trailers in front of the cinemas, music from the shops and people with radios. I could not hear it but I could sense it was very much alive and feel the energy. I got greasy from the food but I just thought who the hell cares. I felt that anything could happen and for the first time I felt positive about coming to London. It was an attitude of: 'Let's see what the next few weeks will bring.'

On the Sunday before rehearsals started Elizabeth decided she wanted to see the sea. She and Jean Worth left Victoria Station by train to spend the day in Brighton. The Southern Region train took her by surprise with its compartments, upholstered seats, sliding doors and curtains — all in direct contrast to the open carriages and more spartan comforts of American trains:

I felt like royalty on that train. It was like something from a movie. I expected Robert Taylor to walk in any minute. Jean and I stopped on the way to the beach at a coffee shop run by an elderly couple who were so nice. We had a cheese sandwich and sat at a counter by the window for a long time and no-one bothered us. We talked more personally than we had ever done before. She was telling me about her family and we talked about self-improvement. She told me I must be less suspicious and more trustful with people. It was like she was preparing me for what lay ahead.

They walked to the sea front and Elizabeth could hardly believe how much it resembled the West Haven beach she had known as a child. There were more stones on the Brighton beach but there were the same two piers and amusement stalls. With Newhaven just down the coast she wondered if the creators of West Haven had found their inspiration in Sussex. The two women walked endlessly (despite the constant drizzle which fulfilled Elizabeth's expectation of English weather) and returned to London with new heart.

Elizabeth's introduction to the Mermaid Theatre that first Monday morning did not encourage her:

> Everyone said it was a beautiful theater but it was not my idea of beautiful. I had heard so much about the Old Vic and I thought it might be that sort of atmosphere but it wasn't. It had just been rebuilt and I thought it was all brick and very cold.

She did not have time to concern herself for long with her new working environment. Waiting for her were the director, Gordon Davidson, Trevor Eve and the rest of the cast. Two American hard-of-hearing actors, Ed Kelly and Julianne Gold, had been brought over from the New York production to play the radical student Orin and the busybody Lydia. The three remaining actors were English and unused to deaf theatre and ASL. They were John Graham as the college principal, Irene Sutcliffe as Sarah Norman's mother and Joan Blackham as the lawyer.

Trevor Eve arrived for the first rehearsal fairly bursting to plunge himself into the work that lay ahead. Tall, fair-haired and good-looking, he had been an award-winning student at RADA, started his theatre career in Liverpool and found his West End feet playing Paul McCartney in the Beatles musical, *John, Paul, George, Ringo and Bert*. He had caught Lord Olivier's eye and been cast in a television play directed by him, since then playing opposite him in a recent film remake of *Dracula*. Eve had by now achieved national popularity playing the private investigator hero of the television series, *Shoestring*: he had deliberately waited to find the right play with which to return to the stage. He had turned down the offer of star billing on a national tour and declined an offer of two plays from the Royal Shakespeare Company's artistic director Trevor Nunn before *Children* came along. He was already known in the business as a strong and opinionated actor.

Eve had spent two months in New York learning ASL from Jean Worth and watching the Broadway production of *Children*, and had been consulted on the choice of actress to play Sarah Norman in London: 'I thought the qualities needed for the actress were really someone who was tremendously attractive but not in a superficial way. I had seen the show in the States but what I had missed was a blinding magnetism between Sarah and James. Phyllis, I gather, was giving the New York actor a bad time. I had met her and Linda Bove and had been given the low-down on someone who was playing it on the Coast. I had seen Elizabeth at an understudy rehearsal and she stood out to me as having all the qualities. She was attractive and a very expressive person with a real quality on the stage. When I was asked my opinion I said there was only one — Elizabeth.'

Trevor Eve's imagination and competitive spirit had been fired by the problems he knew he would have to face: 'From the first time I read it I had been gripped by what seemed this impossible thing. When I saw it in New York I thought: "What a role. What a challenge." Those sort of opportunities are very rare and too good to miss. I was excited by the whole thing. I knew there would be difficulties. The sign language does not exactly match speech. It becomes naturalistic and colloquial. The problem was speaking verbally and signing at the same time when the two were not exactly matching each other. I had got the sign language under my belt by the time we started rehearsal and was able to work on the role, work on the play. I somehow felt that no-one had quite cracked the play. I wanted to find the depth, get to the play, the character, find the connections and communicate that to the audience.' Pippa Ailion noticed Eve's eager determination: 'Trevor could not wait to get started. I had never seen an actor so well prepared to start work on a play.'

Gordon Davidson began rehearsals with a meeting of the cast to explain his intentions. He was not going to duplicate the New York show but, in his own words, to re-originate it. That statement opened a yawning pit of terror in Elizabeth as she remembered her previous failures in the creative process of theatre in America. But there was a temporary reprieve that first day, which the company spent getting to know each other as they worked on the lines and moves of the play. Elizabeth went home relieved that the first day was over but also knowing that there were now only four weeks exactly to the official first night. Davidson recalls: 'That first part was fairly easy. We got the play on its feet, we shaped it and the actors were all very willing. Then we had to start to go back over it and dig a little deeper. That's when the going got tough and things became a little difficult and volatile.'

The pattern was established that Davidson would work with Elizabeth and Trevor Eve during the mornings then the rest of the cast would join them in the afternoon. Those morning sessions became the sheerest hell Elizabeth had ever known.

> I spent most of the first two weeks in tears. I was terrified. They wanted to improvise their way into the play and I had no idea how to do it. I had hidden behind Phyllis's characterization before but Gordon was not going to let me do that now. I wanted to make it my own but I didn't know if I could do it and I was too afraid to try. Gordon kept urging me on but it was no good. Trevor was very forceful. He would come at me with an idea saying, 'Let's try this', and I could not respond. I just retreated and started crying again.

Elizabeth prayed for the afternoons to arrive when the pressure would be taken off her by the arrival of the rest of the cast. At the end of each day she left the theatre emotionally exhausted to pour out her anxieties to Jean Worth at the Baker Street flat or return alone to St John's Wood. She went to buy books on acting theory and technique to see if they could provide an answer but they were no help. As her own self-doubt increased she began to question the friends around her. She did not know if she was right to trust Davidson whom she had known only slightly in New York; she did not know if she should trust Trevor Eve, despite the fact that she had liked him initially; and she even began to doubt her closest companion, Jean Worth. Most of all she did not know if she could trust herself to produce the performance they required, and the first night was coming nearer.

Jean Worth saw what was happening: 'There was a great load on Liz and she went into rehearsals frightened. With little experience of her own, she was starting work with professionals and was missing the support team of Billy and the family. In the early stages, rehearsals were moving slowly, not least because Liz did not understand the rehearsal process and character development. Trevor would be exploring, trying to hit a moment or find a route to make a scene work and Liz was not picking up the cue from him. She seemed completely at a loss. She just didn't understand much of what was going on. I could talk to her afterwards about her anxieties and pain but there was nothing I could actually do about it.'

The more Davidson and Eve pressed her to respond, the more Elizabeth drew into herself and was unable to join them in their exploratory way of working:

It was very difficult at first. I felt some people might be babying me. I'd seen all that before, the toothy smiles and the baby talk and I did not like it. Nobody could tell me exactly what to do, nor could they do it for me. I had to come out and grab hold of it myself and both Gordon and Trevor were helpless, waiting for something to happen. I knew exactly what was going on and every time I failed in those early days the anguish within me grew. I understood very clearly what I was supposed to do, what they were saying and what my rôle was but I just could not open up and do it. I was afraid of making a fool of myself. Trevor was rough. I hated him. I really could not stand him. I felt as if I was the most unfortunate Sarah Leeds of all having to work with someone like that. He was trying something new all the time because he was so passionately committed to the play and he was trying to make me snap out of it, trying to shake me out of my shell. Every time I failed to deliver I would feel worse because I knew it was not Trevor's fault or Gordon's, it was me. That is what made me break down and cry. I knew they were being rough because they wanted me to come through.

But all the time I wanted to get rid of the little girl in me who was so good at making excuses for not doing the things that I knew I could do but did not want to do. Gordon would imitate me — stand the way I was standing at rehearsals, arms folded, face defiant, closed, watchful and detached. I hated those impersonations. It was humiliating, but it was necessary. If he had not done that I do not think I would ever have woken up. He knew that if you leave someone alone they will never grow. What made it so painful for me was that I do have a good imagination. I am very creative but that part of me was clashing with my terrible insecurity which is all based on my lack of formal training. But I do have the right instincts. I know what is good.

I knew coming to London that things were going to be different. It was not just my whole lack of technique and experience in rehearsal. In deaf theater, I had always been pampered and given special attention by the director. They always took care of me and I was spoiled. This time I was going to have to do it for myself. But I was getting desperate. I felt so exposed, so fragile. I could easily have quit. The experience could have finished me off. I was paranoid with fear. I kept thinking of my father and his advice that each day is a new day and somehow that kept me going. I stuck with it.

Trevor Eve made an effort to make things easier for them all:

He would say sometimes that he found his own lines difficult. I think he meant it. He was trying to make me see that I wasn't the only one.

Nonetheless, in the face of rather slow progress, tensions and frustrations which had gone unexpressed before came to the surface. Suspecting hostility, Elizabeth became less co-operative rather than more so. Once or twice, she even accused Jean Worth of not interpreting correctly what she was saying, or what Davidson was trying to say to her:

It was a way to fight back. I was terrible to Jean, really rotten to her. I could not take it out on Gordon or Trevor but I could take it out on her — and I did. If I did not fight back over the interpreting, I would just get out and go to my room.

The conflicts of the play were beginning to be mirrored in rehearsals; the deaf and hearing worlds were not coming together and the misunderstandings and misconceptions caused by the language barrier increased the tension in the Mermaid's third-floor rehearsal room. Jean Worth said: 'Trevor had a very expressive face and Liz would respond to that. If he had a severe expression, she would think he was angry and respond to that, even though his voice showed warmth and concern. The connections were misfiring left, right and centre.' Gordon Davidson also understood what was happening but it was beyond his control: 'The paranoia in deaf people is very high. In translating attitudes, concepts and ideas, the understanding is not always absolutely clear. For example, someone might have a complaint, someone else would ask why were they bitching and the deaf person might end up thinking they were being called a bitch. That is the sort of thing that happened.'

Trevor Eve admits in retrospect that he was prepared to force the pace in rehearsals: 'I was very excited about working with Liz. The play is a love story. It is important to be able to love that girl, to establish the fact that this man can't live his life without her. Liz had the ability to make that possible. She had a presence. When she started rehearsal she realised what she had let herself in for and I think it quite hit her. I was looking for a motivational sort of work in rehearsal. We were trained actors and Elizabeth had not worked with actors in that way before. The rehearsal process was new to her. The theatre is not a comfortable couch. Whatever happens you are going to open on that first night. We were like a couple of animals in a ring startling each other. The director would ask what was going on, why are you doing that and she developed a sort of paranoia. It wasn't anything aimed at her. It was because of the play. Rehearsal can be an emotional process and sometimes a painful one. There is an intensity. It excites me and at times it did become a highly intense situation. Liz would get defensive. I love commitment. What made me come on stronger than her was that I knew something could happen. I knew it could work. There was also a little bit of British pride at stake. I was determined to make it work and show it could be done as well in London as in America and if possible even a little bit better.'

It was Gordon Davidson's responsibility to impose some form of productive order on what was fast slipping into chaos: 'There came a time when we had to sort out what was real and honest and what games were being played. We had a concentrated situation with an actor and an actress in demanding roles bringing their ego and self-protection with them. That was complicated by the problems of communication between the deaf and hearing worlds and how they relate to each other. Liz somehow had to free herself of her insecurity but in the meantime we got to know that at that stage her personal style as an individual and as an actress was quiet rebellion. She was very capable of being hurt and also of acting like a little child. Trevor could be a total pain in the ass and he could be wonderful but I felt that everything he was doing in those early stages was in the service of the play. I knew that James Leeds was a hellishly difficult part. He had to take on the responsibility of the play and be the voice of the actress who is almost bound to get more attention than he does. He also has to play his own character. When before had an actor ever been asked to do something like that? I also knew that the play worked best when Sarah and James make demands on each other. When they are right there in the boxing ring. James has to want to make her over as a mirror image of himself. It then becomes his defeat, his attempt to break her, and that makes it the more frightening. It was something we had to go through but I did begin to wonder if we were going to make it.'

Tempers continued to flare, even when Elizabeth came near to providing the sort of rehearsal that was expected of her:

> We were working on the bedroom scene where James Leeds climbs in through Sarah's window. I invented a door in the set. It was an improvization and Gordon told me to do it. But I froze. I couldn't do it. Trevor lost patience again. He exploded. Gordon pushed me on and said I had to do it but I just cried.

A fortnight into rehearsals Elizabeth's attitude started to change as she found the nerve to haul herself out of the deep well of her own insecurity:

I don't know how I kept going through those two weeks. Apart from what was happening during the day I had gone through sleepless nights worrying about it all. But there must have been something deep inside me knowing I could do it. That ball of courage must have been bigger than I thought. In the middle of rehearsals I began to get the feeling: 'I see. It's all right. I just have to open up and give. Gordon is right there and Trevor will help me.' I was ready to have a go and see what came out.

The breakthrough came in a scene in which Sarah Norman is goaded by James Leeds into defending her communication skills and turns on him with a defiant speech:

I understood that it was OK to open up, to try something and let go and be wild. I started the speech and it was me coming through. Nothing like it had happened to me before. I was putting myself into it. I came through and gave Sarah Norman life but instead of me becoming Sarah it was Sarah becoming me. The look on Trevor's face was incredible. He seemed stunned at what I was doing. I was shocked at what I was saying and doing. They were honest feelings coming through. It felt like a triumph for me, an achievement.

The scene continued unbroken as Sarah tells James that he can never enter her world and that deafness is not just the opposite of hearing, but a silence full of sound:

Trevor very genuinely came up to me and the whole scene began to flow. I could feel Sarah melting and feeling a genuine love for James. I really felt that I was able to share with him my sound of silence. It started with a plateau stretching on and on, bare and rocky, and then the plateau begins to break up and to dissolve and a different image forms, uncertain first and then clearer. It is a horse galloping by the side of a stormy sea. The horse is wild and the waves are wild. And then, gradually, the tumult subsides and the light softens and the scene is transformed into one of serenity and tranquillity. James is amazed that Sarah has shared this with him. I was amazed that it had come from me. I had allowed myself to come out into the open and to understand the depth and the substance of the character. When it was over Gordon was excited and said it had been wonderful. Jean said it was the best scene I had done, then she told me that Gordon had said I was beginning to function as an actress.

Elizabeth was on her way at last and, though there was still the occasional moment of tension, rehearsals could pick up a new impetus to take the company towards their opening night. Elizabeth had found not just a route into playing Sarah but a whole method of working which had not been available before.

At last I had found a way to work. I knew I could trust other people and, most important, that I could trust myself. I had learned to be less insecure, that it was all right to make a fool of yourself. Trevor was wonderful with me, encouraging me, after that scene. He had been after me for two weeks and I had finally done it. He had come on strong and been impossible at times but I was pleased he had. Despite the pain, I would not have had it any other way. He had shaken me out of it.

The rehearsals swept on in a new atmosphere. Elizabeth showed her new command of the important speech to the Commission — a speech on which she had been working since she first used it as an audition piece — and, together, she and Trevor Eve mastered the technically complex matter of synchronising his delivery with Elizabeth's signing to catch the rhythm and exact expression of the speech. They were able to work on refining the characters and bringing the piece to a unity. Elizabeth was able to assemble a new interpretation of Sarah free from the shadow of Phyllis Frelich's performance, adding her own sensitivity and vulnerability as well as her own attractive physical presence.

Davidson watched with approval as Elizabeth grew into the role: 'Liz has a size and luminosity on the stage which I think is God-given. She gave Sarah such stature. More than any other Sarah I saw, she brought a kind of innocence and true naivety. I think her instinct had more of that rather than the hurt and injustice others had. Liz is also a romantic and that sense of romance is crucial to the play.' As Elizabeth says:

After all that time copying Phyllis I had to go right down into myself to inject those feelings into Sarah this time. It was hard because I have had that repressed anger of hers and always felt so much of an outsider and alone when everyone else was part of a togetherness. But there was also the sense of humour and caring which was in Sarah. I think that is what Gordon liked. I dug into myself and just unzipped and everything fell out — my insecurity, my fear, my defensiveness, everything.

Rehearsals moved down to the stage in the third week of rehearsal and this was a blessing for Elizabeth after her ordeal upstairs. The first preview was a private affair given to 300 Friends of the theatre who could be relied on to be a supportive audience. Trevor Eve warned her that from then on all their work would be done in public:

I was eager to get in front of an audience. I wanted to know from them what was good in the play, what was working. I wanted to know if we could communicate everything we wanted to. I had grown enormously in the past two weeks and I wondered how I would feel in front of an audience and how we would all be received. Going on in front of them made me give everything I could. It was hard work, which is what Trevor had meant, but it was worth it. On stage I discovered how good Trevor was. He had been great in rehearsal but on stage he was amazing. I knew James Leeds was going to work and that I had helped him towards it but I did not know if I was going to get on the same level myself.

The remaining previews were sold out as London's most ardent theatre fans flocked to see the latest Broadway hit. Each night the audience gave the play and its performers a rousing ovation and the rapport between Elizabeth and Trevor Eve grew.

The day of the first night arrived at last, with its sickening dawn start for Elizabeth. The silent prayer to her father in the wings and the sudden burst of energy when she took her place on the stage sustained her through the performance to the ovation which marked her personal triumph. Then on to the first-night party and the 2.00 a.m. return to St John's Wood where the memory of the cheering audience moved her to thoughts of the sea and joy at the new-found strength she had discovered.

Elizabeth slept until early afternoon the next day while others concerned themselves with the Press excitement the play had caused. The producers and managers devoured glowing reviews which guaranteed a successful run at the Mermaid Theatre and a transfer to the West End thereafter. The Mermaid box office was under siege and took a record amount in advance bookings. At his Chiswick home, a philosophical Trevor Eve took the morning papers to a park bench by the Thames. He had been properly acclaimed for his performance but he noticed that it was Elizabeth who had captured the headlines. He said later: 'It was predictable, I suppose, that the Press would go for the phenomenon of a deaf girl acting on the stage and I had expected it, but I thought some of them missed the centre of the play.'

It was late afternoon when Elizabeth arrived at the theatre for the second evening's performance and now the impact of the London premiere of *Children* became apparent to her. Ed Kelly had a complete set of the morning papers and the Mermaid's press officer, Claire Thornton, had the London evening paper, the *Standard*, which carried a photograph of Elizabeth on the front page, an inside story headlined, *'London's new star takes a silent bow — audience acclaim for the actress who can't hear a word'*, and a glowing review further back in the paper. The press officer told Elizabeth that it was most unusual for a first night to make the front pages. In her dressing room Gordon Davidson and Mark Medoff came to repeat their congratulations of the night before and told her that the papers were all for her:

> They said it as though it was my fault. I probably got it wrong but at the time I thought they were saying I wasn't that good but the papers had liked me anyway. Then they said Trevor was feeling down. I told them I could not have done it without Trevor. They said I should tell him that, so all three of us went into his dressing room. I said I was sorry about the papers and repeated that I could not have done it without him.

Trevor Eve signed, 'Me, too', moving his hand between them, and the two fell into a hug. Elizabeth had still not actually read the reviews.

The next morning Elizabeth called in at her local newsagent and was surprised to be greeted effusively by the staff. 'You did not tell us you were an actress,' they said and congratulated her on her triumph. She wanted to get the previous day's papers and the staff went to no little trouble to find a complete set with five copies of each newspaper which Elizabeth just managed to carry back to her apartment. Spreading the reviews out over a table, she started to cut out the notices to send home to her family. This was when she read her own notices for the first time and they made good reading.

The *Daily Mail* said:

Without saying a word on stage for more than two hours, Elizabeth Quinn reached out to the audience and scooped it into the palm of her hand last night. The deaf actress could not hear the thunderous applause but when she saw all those hands clapping her, it was the kind of sign language she had been waiting to see. More eloquent than words, her performance as the deaf girl who falls in love with the speech therapist who is trying to make her talk instead of using sign language communicates an inner longing for normality that is heart-breaking. This mighty Quinn can have you laughing with her one moment and shedding tears for her the next as she fights for an independence from the isolation of her silent world on terms she dictates herself.

The *Daily Express* critic wrote:

As Sarah, Elizabeth Quinn — who is herself deaf — gives a perform-ance hard to forget. She communicates entirely in sign language. Only twice does she break her otherwise total silence — once to let us hear a muffled sobbing and once in a terrifying explosion of great dramatic force.

The Times:

The heroine is marvellously played by Elizabeth Quinn ... her physical dignity, intelligence and the sheer authority of her person-ality are such that she holds the whip hand from the moment she sets foot on stage.

The *Financial Times:*

The performance of Elizabeth Quinn, who reveals her political conscience in a mesmerising display of sign language as part of the character's defiance, is amazing.

The *Daily Telegraph*:

The performance of Elizabeth Quinn is as absorbing as the twinkling dance of her restless fingers as she flirts and quarrels in sign language.

In *The Standard*, Milton Shulman wrote:

Elizabeth Quinn with every movement of her body and every flick of her darting eyes indicates a defiance of the hearing world that is arrogant, awesome and admirable.

> I was amazed at some of the things that had been written but I was proud of them. They had written of the things I was trying to convey. It was not just people saying you were wonderful but being specific, which is what I wanted. I was astounded at my own achievement. It made clear to me the fact that I could get through to an audience. I understood what it was to communicate something to them, that you have to have a private conversation with every one of them. It finally convinced me that I was doing the right thing and acting was what I did best. I was on the right road.

TWELVE

A Long Run

Children of a Lesser God settled into its run at the Mermaid Theatre as one of the hottest show in town, playing to capacity audiences. Gordon Davidson, Mark Medoff and other Americans who had arrived for the opening returned to the United States and the show was established in its own routine. Elizabeth's life was turned around in more ways than one. The success of her first night and the novelty for London of having a deaf actress on one of its stages made her an object of considerable media interest. She was regularly interviewed by newspapers and magazines and frequently disappointed by the inaccuracy with which she was reported. She also received a constant stream of fan mail with many letters from members of the audience who simply wanted to reiterate their thanks for her performance as they felt Elizabeth would not have been aware of their applause.

It got to the point where Elizabeth could not keep up with it on her own because she likes to reply to every letter personally; so the management recruited Joan Pritchett to work with her for two weeks:

> Two weeks turned into two years and Joan became more than a secretary. I feel I can really be myself with Joan. She has a sense of humour, she gets things into perspective, she never babies me but, like Billy, can let me know what people really mean behind the words they use. Faced with the problem of having to dictate letters to someone, I was worried about whether I could express myself but Joan just sat there and waited so I had to say something, which was good for me. Joan does not sign or read sign at all so that was one of the best things that could happen to me. I have

watched Joan handle both her own career as a writer and her family and because we are so close and have shared so much, I can see how strong she is and it gives me hope that one day I too will be able to handle both a career and a family.

It proved an invaluable partnership for Joan Pritchett also: 'I am glad I met Elizabeth. She is the sort of person who makes you feel better for being in their company, and that is rare. Elizabeth has taught me a lot about communication, about the value of words, because what she says is what she means. And it is impossible not to be equally honest and straightforward with her. Above all Elizabeth is gloriously funny, down-to-earth, and she takes life at a gallop. I like that. Since getting to know her, not only I, but my whole family, have benefited from her friendship.'

After a month of rehearsing by day and fleeing to the sanctuary of her apartment in the evening, Elizabeth's practice now was to rest by day and conserve her energy for the evening's show. The draining tension of the rehearsals had been replaced by the physical demands on energy and stamina of playing the show six nights a week plus two afternoon matinees. It was the customary theatrical schedule but one which was new to her as a permanent way of working. The likelihood of a transfer to the West End grew ever stronger with the implicit message to Elizabeth that her stay in London would be longer than she had anticipated. The Albery Theatre in St Martin's Lane (directly across the road from the Laguna restaurant where the first-night party had been held) was identified as the next likely home for *Children*. Elizabeth started asking discreet questions about the theatre. Was it much bigger than the Mermaid? What reputation did it have for plays? Which actors had appeared there before? The answers confirmed that she had hit the front line of British theatre and she took no comfort from that, quite the opposite.

The Albery Theatre was a plush, post-Victorian house of 900 seats with a distinguished past going back to the turn of the century. Laurence Olivier and Ralph Richardson had run the

Old Vic Company from there in the 1940s, turning out regularly on its stage. Olivier had returned there more recently for O'Neill's *Long Day's Journey into Night* (the television version of which Elizabeth had watched in West Haven) and the theatre stars who had appeared there subsequently included Ingrid Bergman, Dame Wendy Hiller, Diana Rigg, Dorothy Tutin, Judi Dench, Donald Sinden and Deborah Kerr. Before she could allow herself to be unsettled at the thought of following in such prestigious footsteps, Elizabeth still had six weeks at the Mermaid to negotiate:

> My life seemed very limited. The theatre was all I was doing. Playing every night and keeping it fresh every night was exhausting. I used to sleep until the afternoon and then go to the theater. The only good moment was at the end of each show when you saw how the audience appreciated the play. Joan Blackham said that when I went to take my curtain call I ran on like the happiest girl in the world. It was true. But after that all I had was the lonely road home. I never felt like a star or anything like that. I never digested the success of it all. I still felt very unsure about this new set-up.

An unfortunate by-product of the publicity she was receiving came when a couple of publications described Elizabeth as deaf and dumb. The use of the word 'dumb', with its American connotation of stupidity as well as its inaccuracy in her case, hurt her deeply and forced her to ask herself if she should begin to use her voice. Interviewers tended to pay more attention to her interpreter than to herself which made it hard for her to express herself as she wished to. But she was not yet ready to use her voice and the only words she spoke at the Mermaid were in occasional conversations with Trevor Eve. For all that they achieved on stage together, the actor and the actress were not always in total agreement:

> The show was different every night. Some nights one scene would be the best, another night it would be another scene. I always wanted it all to be the best. Trevor and I

were up and down. We had disagreements. He never once came into my dressing room. I always had to go into his room. But I could always talk things out with Trevor. I liked that. If we had a row we did not leave the theater until it was sorted out. Sometimes we were there until midnight and would be the last to leave.

Midway through the Mermaid run, the move to the Albery Theatre was announced. Posing as a curious tourist, Elizabeth went to the theatre and asked to be allowed to look inside. She was recognised instantly and escorted on a tour of the theatre, then left to sit alone in the royal circle. Mesmerised by the gilt and red plush, she sat and tried to picture herself and the rest of the cast on the stage in front of her. Then one free Sunday, when Elizabeth set off by Underground to visit Covent Garden, she emerged from one of the many exits at Leicester Square station to be confronted by a vast sign painted on a wall, saying, *'CHILDREN OF A LESSER GOD — THIS WAY'*, accompanied by a large arrow. Startled, she followed the arrow to the back of the Albery Theatre:

I walked down the alley and saw the stage door. The scenery dock was open and I could see the crew setting up on stage. They were working so hard, I wanted to go down and help them. They were just as much part of the play as I was: the crew are the lifeblood of the theater. I walked round the front and they had the front-of-house marquee up with a huge picture of Trevor and me. It was so big. I was amazed and stood in the street shaking. I wanted to apologize for it and say it is only me. I did not think I deserved it. Not me, the girl from the beach who is lazy and undisciplined. I walked round Covent Garden but I could not get that sight out of my mind. Not even Phyllis had had anything like that.

Gordon Davidson returned for a week's rehearsal to set the show on the Albery stage and it was he who first took her to see her new dressing room. The room was large and airy with its own refrigerator and assorted furniture and the director suggested she could live there if she so chose.

Before leaving the Mermaid, Elizabeth attended the dress rehearsal of a deaf and hearing production of Peter Schaffer's hit play *Equus* at the Young Vic Theatre. Lewis Merkin, who had originated the role of Orin in *Children*, had travelled from America to London to take a leading role. Elizabeth was impressed by the courage with which her hard-of-hearing friend took a spoken role on stage but she also noticed a solitary figure watching the rehearsal. He was a British actor, Richard O'Callaghan, well known to London audiences from plays at the Royal Court and in the West End, where he was currently playing Mozart in *Amadeus*. Elizabeth had been told of the power of that performance and made sure she was introduced to him. Mr O'Callaghan created a very favourable impression.

Elizabeth bade a sad farewell to the Mermaid, feeling that she was yet again being uprooted from a familiar environment, and prepared for the first night at the Albery. After the extra rehearsals and wear and tear of the move, the cast did not feel they gave of their absolute best that night, but a crowd of celebrating friends and visitors soon filled Elizabeth's dressing room after the show. Producer Ian Albery found her to say that she would be appearing in his theatre for a long time to come.

For Elizabeth in particular, there were daunting changes to get used to:

> The Albery was the biggest theater I had ever performed in, except for those two weeks at the Longacre Theater in New York. Because the audience seemed so far away I felt cut off from them, especially when we were taking our bows. I could not see them at all at first. It was pitch black and I did not know who I was bowing to. They experimented with the lighting ... finally they came up with a dim light and that seemed to work. It is important to me to be able to see the audience. That was what was so good about the Mermaid. I knew, as we guided them through the story, that they were getting the message and I appreciated that.

To help her maintain good contact with the audience, Elizabeth's dresser, Jon Jon, established a special routine which

continued throughout her run. In the quick changes during the
performance, he would tell her how the audience was
responding:

> Jon Jon had the script in his hands and he would mark it
> for me, writing either 1, 2 or 3. One meant pretty good, 2
> meant very good and 3 meant fantastic. He also wrote
> down if they were clapping and he would tell me if there
> was someone out there laughing louder than everyone else,
> and whereabouts they were sitting, so I would know. Quite
> often if I came off and Jon Jon said it was only No.1 then I
> would go back on and I knew I had to try to pick it up and
> get that response back to No.2 or No.3.

Shortly after they opened at the Albery, the theatre's publicity
representative told Elizabeth that she had been approached to
see if Elizabeth and Trevor Eve might go on the Russell Harty
television chat show. Harty and his production associates would
be coming to see the play and it was arranged that they would
meet Elizabeth and Trevor after the performance:

> Russell Harty and his colleagues came back after the show
> and they seemed elated with it. But then there was a
> muddle over whose dressing room we were meeting in. It
> was so embarrassing. We all moved but I was putting up
> my defences. I was hurt and humiliated and getting
> uptight. Russell Harty was uncomfortable with me.
> Trevor was his usual charming self and I must have looked
> like a witch. I could not believe what was going on. Jean
> told me to let it blow over but I couldn't. Russell Harty
> asked me if I was prepared to talk about my deafness on his
> show and I said I would not, that I was not handicapped.
> But it was decided that we would do the show. Then
> Russell said the most poignant moment in the play had
> been when I said I wanted deaf babies. That specific detail
> pleased me as we had been working on that. I melted a
> little.

The question was raised of whether Elizabeth might use her
voice on the television show. Jean Worth urged her to speak but
the producer Ian Albery argued against it as he believed a

public knowledge that Elizabeth could speak might alter the audience's conception and appreciation of the play. Elizabeth was still not sure that she was ready to use her voice in public and agreed not to do so.

A week later a car collected Elizabeth and Jean Worth to take them to the studio, where the show would be televised live. Russell Harty met Elizabeth in the dressing room and with his usual charm put her at her ease:

> This was my first talk show, like Johnny Carson in the States. I had borrowed a dress for it. When Trevor and I were in the hospitality room we were both shaking. Trevor went on first and he talked very well then I had to go on. It went well. I was quick and sharp. At one point, Harty asked me if I had a companion. I said, 'My God, this isn't "The Miracle Worker"!' I felt I was a spokesperson for deaf people. Harty said I talked too much but I told him that was what he had told me to do. The show had a big response and a good reaction. I had a lot of letters and many people who saw the program came to see the play.

Days turned into weeks as the open-ended run at the Albery Theatre continued to draw the crowds but the pressures of sustaining their demanding performance began to tell on both Elizabeth and Trevor Eve. The effort of transforming the nightly routine of another performance into a live and organic event for the audience was a taxing one. Elizabeth went on stage one evening to find that in place of the adrenalin and imagination which fuelled her performance there was — nothing. Convinced that the audience would notice the flatness of her performance, she toiled her way through the play. When she reached the speech to the Commission she prayed for some feeling, some impetus to touch her but still she felt a void. When the curtain was down she told Trevor Eve what had happened, how empty she had felt. He reassured her and said the same thing had happened to himself. Her performance had been fine and the audience had responded as they usually did. For the first time, she had survived the show on technique alone without calling on the emotional resources she used to charge each scene; it was not her preferred way of working, but it was good to know that the safety net was there.

For Trevor Eve, the strain of carrying the responsibilities of the James Leeds role was great and sometimes caused erratic behaviour: 'The play became very difficult. After the Mermaid, I began to get very insular and introverted. I had to develop my concentration. It was a really hard show to do. I had given it so much concentration during the rehearsals that I went into myself. I never really relaxed through the whole run. Every night before I went on I would lock myself in the dressing room and warm up with the signing. I never once felt that the play could carry itself. I played James Leeds for eight months in all. I did nothing else in that time except every night after the show I would go home and run a couple of videos. The play was not always a pleasurable experience. After the opening the director was out of the country. There was no-one coming back to the show to have a good yell at us for what we were doing. It was strange. There were always two camps, two worlds. It was not just a question of actors and actresses together. There were the two worlds of the deaf and the hearing and the play and life itself became difficult to separate.'

It was true that Gordon Davidson, with his own theatre to run in Los Angeles, was only a rare visitor to London once the production was established but he knew what was happening: 'We did hit that peak of excitement when we opened. The miracle for me was that we did bring it together and I think it held. To this day I believe some of the most exciting work that took place on *Children* was for the London production. I enjoyed myself in that top room at the Mermaid. I think it is true that, after opening, Trevor did have problems coping with the run and feeling himself a star but it was terrific that we had him. He was always very demanding and would never settle for anything. He wanted to work past what was given him, to go further. He and Rubinstein were the two best James Leeds I ever saw.'

The director was also aware of Elizabeth's continuing progress: 'One of the greatest pleasures for me was the way Liz broke through. She really had to work on herself to get free of that insecurity thing. Towards the opening night she did beat it. I am not sure she had completely beat it by that first night. It went on from there. She showed she could be tough. Achieving what she did took a lot of doing and watching her do it was exhilarating.'

The two actors received the fresh encouragement they needed in November 1981 when formal letters arrived at the Albery stage door to tell them they had been nominated for best actor and best actress in the Society of West End Theatre Awards. First they had to attend an informal ceremony at the Society's offices to receive an inscribed scroll commemorating their nomination, then there would be a glossy Sunday night presentation dinner for 1000 people at the Café Royal during which the awards would be announced. *Nominated!* The very word, with its association with Hollywood's Academy Awards, was enough for Elizabeth, whether she won the award or not — and the more so when she learned that she had been bracketed with two of England's finest actresses, Maggie Smith and Eileen Atkins. She rang home to tell her mother and Billy the news.

When the day of the presentation ceremony arrived, Jean Worth booked a hairdresser to visit her flat and attend to both of them — Jean ended up with her hair piled up on one side of her head and Elizabeth emerged with a mass of dark curls. To relieve the tension Jean opened a bottle of champagne: 'I was sozzled by the time we set off.' During the dinner Elizabeth tried to find Dutch courage from the wine on the table but was too nervous to drink at all. Russell Harty went up on stage to announce the best actress award and Elizabeth lip-read him as he said '... and the winner is Miss Elizabeth Quinn.'

People starting standing up and Jean popped up with her hair swaying on her head. I was crying and laughing at the same time at the sight of Jean's tipsy hair. I walked through the tables to the stage and looked round at the sea of faces and everyone was applauding. It was like opening

night again with the same sense of approval. I had to wait
until the applause died down then all of a sudden Jean was
standing by me saying: 'Would you like to say a few words,
Elizabeth?' She was wobbly, her hair was wobbly and her
signing was wobbly. I was laughing and trying to make
myself believe it was really happening. I handed the award
to Jean so I could sign but after a few words I had to stop
because the audience were applauding so much they could
not hear Jean. I walked down the steps off stage. I forgot
the award and Jean carried it for me as she walked behind,
swaying gently.

Trevor Eve received the best actor award and *Children* was voted
best play — the London run was matching the play's New York
success exactly. To crown it all, Lord Olivier was at the dinner
to present a special award to Sir Ralph Richardson and at the
end of the event Trevor Eve introduced Elizabeth to him.

There was an inevitable sense of anti-climax the next day
when the routine of life returned. Letters and messages of
congratulation arrived by the dozen at the theatre but Elizabeth reflected soberly that awards, however splendid to receive,
were of no real significance. The degree of professional recognition she had received was of less importance than the development she knew she still needed in her personal life. The first
task she set herself was to begin using her own voice:

Even though I was frightened I was determined to begin to
speak to people, to move around socially in the hearing
world and to deal with people on a business level too. I
knew I would not always get it right, I would be saying the
wrong thing at the wrong time, that some people would
get hurt and that I would be hurt too. My resolve was
strengthened when I went to a dinner given by Ray
Cooney for the casts of his plays. We were all at a long table
and for the first time in England I was alone in a group of
hearing people. I watched them eating, talking and laughing with their lips moving and their heads turning to each
other and turning away still talking and I wanted to be
part of that. I felt very much an outsider. They were so
confident and so much at ease with each other. They all
had their own personalities but none of them knew me at

all and there was no way they were going to know me if I remained cut off from them. The feeling was growing inside me that I had to do something about it. It would be difficult and it would take time but I had to be patient and gradually I would get there. It was going to be painful but I knew that to develop my own character and personality I was going to have to take the most appalling risks. I thought: 'Yes, I'm going to do it.'

The following day Elizabeth and Trevor were locked in another heated row to which Elizabeth brought all the resolution of her new intent. Their exchanges ended with the actor declaring his genuine affection for her:

In front of everyone, Trevor said: 'I like you, Liz. I like you very much.' When he said that I stopped and thought. I realized that what he had said was that there was something in me he liked. Me, Elizabeth. And that was something that I had to bring out and discover for myself — that I had been infecting everything with negative feelings about myself and my own insecurity. We made it up and hugged each other and when I hugged him it was a hug of gratitude and apology. I was sorry it had happened but, to be honest, I was happy it happened too and thankful and I left the theatre with a strange sense of excitement about this new awareness of myself.

Following Elizabeth's SWET award, an interview had been booked with Valerie Grove, a leading journalist on the *Standard*. Elizabeth determined to answer the questions verbally, much to Mrs Grove's surprise, and the feature interview ran under the headline: '*The girl who can speak after all.*' In her article, Valerie Grove wrote:

The fact that she received her award in sign language, and on the stage plays a deaf girl who refuses to learn to utter a word, may mislead people into thinking she cannot speak herself. But she can. She is not only perfectly intelligible, she is quick-witted and articulate. She has given several interviews through a sign-language interpreter. This was, she told me, because she was shy. She has no idea what her voice sounds like. But just lately she has begun to feel brave enough to speak with her own voice. It is a soft and gentle voice, rather a Meryl Streep sort of voice. People in shops often ask if she is French.

It was the first public knowledge that Elizabeth had a speaking voice.

By this time Richard O'Callaghan, the actor Elizabeth had met at the Young Vic, had become quite a friend, escorting her to dinners and parties which took her increasingly into exclusively hearing company. She found herself complimented on her good looks but resented that conversations rarely went beyond that simple courtesy. Jean Worth and Pippa Ailion encouraged her to take the initiative with questions of her own. Richard O'Callaghan said: 'Liz was very nervous at first when we went to meet people. I felt she had no need to be. People were always so pleased to meet her. I was a bit neglectful because I used to forget that Liz was deaf and when we were together we always talked a lot and laughed a lot. I always thought her ability to speak was a miracle. She is so good at it.' But she still took time to feel comfortable with her own voice:

> I was starting to speak and when I was with a group of people standing in a circle I noticed when I was talking that the circle would get smaller. I thought it was because they didn't understand what I was saying but it was because they could not hear me in the noise of the party. My voice was low because I did not have the confidence to speak up. In the early days Richard would repeat after me what I had said so people would know. I didn't like that at all. I used to go hot and red in the face but it wasn't his fault. It was difficult to get the volume right. I was worrying about my grammar because sentence structure is completely different to signed language and pronunciation was another nightmare. But I had got to the point where I could actually ask someone to repeat what they said and I found they did not mind. Before, I had always had to ask somebody else to explain it when I did not understand first time.

From her expeditions into the hearing world with Richard O'Callaghan Elizabeth would return thankfully to the safety of Jean Worth's interpreting services to raise her courage before venturing out again. The constant strain of having to

make that effort combined with the pressure of the show to
sink her into intermittent dark moods until the depression
became so intense that she decided to repeat her Chicago
exercise and go to an analyst. She was pleased to find that the
man she chose to consult knew only the barest details of her
professional life. He led her to re-examine her fears, her lack of
trust in herself, her dissatisfaction with her achievement and the
complexities of her relationships with the members of her
family. She wanted to find answers to why other people per-
ceived her differently from the way she saw herself.

After a Christmas spent with Richard O'Callaghan and his
family Elizabeth proposed a reunion with her own family. Her
mother, Billy and Billy's wife Anita flew to London for a visit to
coincide with Billy's wedding anniversary. They slept off the
effects of their night flight during the afternoon and went to the
Albery Theatre in the evening. Billy recalled: 'When she
walked out on to that stage it was just like the ugly duckling had
turned into a swan. To be honest, I did not like her performance
too much that night. I thought she was not controlled, that she
was going over the top. My feeling was that Trevor was coming
on too strong and she was trying to keep up with him. It was
difficult but I told her what I thought and she seemed to accept
it and to understand. We went back to see her the next night and
it was the best performance I have ever seen her give. She had
made it totally honest.' Billy also noticed the ways in which his
sister's London life had changed her: 'She was dealing with
people in a way I had never seen before. She had the agility to
deal with a number of things at the same time. She just glided
through everything and never missed a beat.'

Elizabeth's analyst took advantage of the family's presence
and invited them to attend one day:

It was a very painful session. He asked me who did I think
my father had loved the most. I had always felt my father
loved me the most and that was why he spent so much time
with me but I found myself saying he loved my mother
most, then my brother, then me and he only spent more
time with me because I was a problem. The therapist

asked my mother and brother if they agreed and though I
hoped they would not they both agreed. At that moment I
saw the West Haven beach where the sea was grey and the
clouds were dark and heavy.

Anita Quinn attended a second session with her daughter
during which they discussed their own relationship:

> That was another session which really got to me and I left
> it breathing very heavily. I finally realized that day how
> strong my mother really was and how unfair I had been to
> her. I had constantly belittled her because I wanted her to
> be more like my father and pay more attention to me but
> she never did. It was the beginning of my respect for her
> and I understood what she had done for the family. It was
> also the beginning of my awareness of myself and my
> ability to be honest with myself. It was another awakening
> for me and an intensely painful one. When my mother
> went back to the States I was glad to be left alone so that I
> could digest what was happening and what I was finding
> out about myself.

Elizabeth was meanwhile being pressed to appear on television
magazine programmes. She went to Birmingham to take part in
a BBC-TV lunchtime programme, 'Pebble Mill at One', at the
end of which the interviewer surprised her by asking her to say a
couple of sentences, which she did. For another programme,
'Nationwide', it was agreed that she would start the interview
signing but then move into speech when the interviewer asked
her about her voice. In the event she conducted the whole
interview vocally while singing at the same time. Despite Jean
Worth's reassurance, she was not convinced that she had
sounded as articulate as she might have wished to but she was
happy to know that she was breaking through.

For both interviews there was a resistance from the producers
of *Children* to the idea of her speaking in public in case it confused
the image of the play but Elizabeth was rewarded with a large
number of supportive and appreciative letters. Some praised
the quality of her voice: 'The inflection and pace is much, much
better than that of the average speaker and the tone so pleasant

and interesting that it was a pleasure to listen to you' — 'We loved your voice. It is soft and full of expression' — 'You have a very attractive voice which matches your whole personality' — 'Your diction was so clear and what amazed me was that you have a lovely, gentle, lilting American accent' — 'It's a great shame you cannot hear your own lovely, husky voice.' (One particular letter, from a singing teacher, simply urged her to use her voice as much as possible: 'Your hand signs are so eloquent, your face so mobile that I can forget someone else is saying the words. [But] when you did venture a few words, the timbre of your voice was melodious and warm, so *please* use it more.') Others admired her determination to speak in public: 'You will be an inspiration to many' — 'Keep on talking, Elizabeth' — 'You can do speaking parts so get on with it and good luck' — 'You are a great encouragement to the many people who are fighting their personal battles in a world that does not always seem to understand or care.'

Elizabeth was also invited to attend public events and, as word of her vocal ability spread, often in a speaking capacity. She was asked to the British Academy of Film and Television Arts annual awards to present the best actor award to Anthony Andrews for his performance in the television serial of 'Brideshead Revisited'. Again she was caught between the reluctance of the play's producers and her own desire to develop her speech. So she signed her presentation speech to Andrews, with Trevor Eve speaking for her. At the end, she leaned towards the microphone to offer one word: 'Congratulations.' She had made her point. At a luncheon for a blind charity she shared a speech with a fellow actor and discovered that, if she treated the audience as just another person with whom she might be in conversation, she could acquit herself more effectively. When she went to a Woman of the Year lunch given by the Variety Club of Great Britain in Leeds she received a best actress award and responded with the succinct speech: 'Thank you for this award. In receiving this honour I can only feel more confident as I make my way in the theater. Last year at the Society of West End Theatre awards I signed, this year I am speaking. If I am lucky enough to get another award I promise I will do a song and dance for you.' She fairly brought the house down.

Trevor Eve's six-month West End contract for *Children* was approaching its end and a replacement had to be found for the James Leeds role. The actor chosen was the tall, dark figure of Oliver Cotton who had recently played Cesare Borgia in the BBC 2 television series of 'The Borgias' but who had an extensive theatre background in the major companies and in the fringe, although he only rarely appeared in the West End. Elizabeth was plunged into a tough new schedule as she rehearsed with her new leading man by day and performed by night. There was no time for any public functions for a while, and she ended her sessions with the analyst and had to forget about any personal life. She also had to learn that actors' techniques and personalities differed; Oliver Cotton's were in direct contrast to Trevor Eve's. Whereas Trevor Eve thrived on commitment and confrontation, Oliver Cotton needed to be led along a gentler path to find his own performance. It was an adjustment which Elizabeth was slow to make and Cotton suffered some discomfort as they worked their way through rehearsals:

> At first I wanted Oliver to be just like Trevor. If there was a problem I wanted to sort it out there and then, as I had done with Trevor. I did not realize how vulnerable Oliver was and I made it extremely difficult for him. It got so bad that Pippa had to come and explain to me what Oliver was feeling. With Trevor I had been able to have a row and then make up but with Oliver I had to find a different method and gradually I learned what a talented and generous actor he was.

The concentration on work had the effect of crystallising Elizabeth's attitudes elsewhere. The strength she had exhibited on Oliver Cotton's arrival and which had provided him with such a challenging welcome she realised now was an in-built part of her emotional armour. Rehearsing by day and playing by night, she was also refining her process of acting:

Pippa told me how forceful I was with people sometimes. I knew I was direct but I wanted people to be direct with me as well. I know that being direct can hurt at times. I do not believe in hurting anyone and I would not want to but I do believe in being honest. That way you know where you are and then you can encourage people. If people ask me a question I tell them what I honestly think. I believe truth is the best way though it does seem to take some people by surprise. In work I am always searching for more honesty and simplicity in my performance and a long time ago I learned that less is more — I believe this is the golden rule in acting.

During the rehearsals with Oliver Cotton, Jean Worth was invited to join a production of *Children* in South Africa where she would act as interpreter and also play the lawyer, Miss Klein. It was an offer she decided to accept. Elizabeth would be losing a friend but also losing the support of having an interpreter available to her. Part of her wanted to rise to that challenge but instead she chose a novel and quite contrasting course of action.

As she watched the rest of the cast go home to the comfort and support of their husbands, wives and lovers, Elizabeth felt the need for a similar kind of companionship. She hit on the idea of bringing Billy and his wife Anita to London to fulfil that need and also to act as her interpreters. She knew that this might return her to her childhood dependence on her brother but hoped that she could hold that at bay and just enjoy his company as a friend. Plans were laid over the trans-Atlantic telephone but were brought to an abrupt halt when Billy announced that Anita was pregnant and they would have to stay in West Haven. Elizabeth felt a strange sense of relief when she heard this news. It was as though she had been helped towards her decision and from now on she would go out into the world without an interpreter. She felt that it was something required of her and she was prepared to take the consequences.

When Oliver Cotton had established himself in the role of James Leeds, Elizabeth was allowed a holiday from the show and chose to go alone to distant and exotic Bali. It was another test she was willing to set herself and one she would survive if only on the basis of trial and error. She took the long flight on her own and was greeted by the local representative of her travel firm, who introduced himself as a prince of the island. Whoever he was, he delighted her by taking her on motor-bike rides around the island and ferrying her to the more remote beaches where she spent long days alone. Her time was taken up with reading actors' biographies, which reassured her that insecurity was an integral part of the profession, and with practising an assertion of will to free herself of the self-inflicted fears and assumed inadequacies which she knew were only holding her back.

Despite the beneficial effects of the holiday, Elizabeth was no sooner home than she suffered a physical and emotional collapse which was diagnosed to her as a delayed reaction to the months of work which had gone before and also a result of the abrupt change of pace when she went to Bali. She was introduced to a homeopathic doctor, Dr Douglas Latto of Harley Street, who took her off work for a week and also took her off the coffee and chocolates which had become staple parts of her diet. The cure worked and, against the advice of Pippa Ailion, Elizabeth returned to *Children* two days ahead of schedule with an appetite for the show she had not felt for a long time:

> It was wonderful to dress in that red jumper and those jeans again, then to walk out on to the stage and wait for the curtain to go up. I felt a momentary nervousness but dismissed it as the unnecessary nuisance it was. When I got down on the stage and felt the music start I could not wait to begin. When Oliver made his exit after our love scene he signed to me: 'It's good to have you back home.' It felt good to me too. Oliver had a marvellous sense of humour and we had a lot of fun during our time together.

The relationship between Elizabeth and Oliver Cotton blossomed during the summer. Undetected, they were able to sign messages to each other on stage and he would guide her on how the audience was responding to the performance. She assumed a positive frame of mind, the show was in good shape and the healthy advance bookings at the box office indicated a long and continuing run.

Part of the satisfaction of playing in *Children* for Elizabeth was the heart-warming response carried to her in letters from members of the audience. Apart from the simple fan mail of admirers wanting photographs (and letters from gentlemen with proposals of marriage), there were many which showed a genuine gratitude for the experience of the play and of her fine performance. One correspondent wrote: 'I must thank you for the most tremendous theatrical experience. I laughed with you and I cried with you. I have rarely been so moved. In fact, I have never felt like this. I still have goose pimples when I think about you playing that demanding part.' Another wrote: 'It is my opinion that it [the performance] is comparable to the best that Dame Margot Fonteyn, our great ballerina, gave through her career in pathos, humour and, at times, tragedy.' From Surrey there came the message: 'You were magical. You reduced me to tears and left me with a lot to think about.' Another theatregoer said: 'Your performance touched our hearts. It wasn't acting, it was real and we should all be grateful to you.' And one male admirer wrote bluntly: 'You're my kind of woman — beautiful, hard-headed and sexy.'

One letter, from a vicar, summed up perhaps more eloquently than others what many sought to say: 'I have never been so moved by a play in my life. You gave so much of what was inside yourself and that was very beautiful. Thank you for being yourself and for being so vulnerable for us who believe that we can hear when really we hear so very little. Thank you for spending so much of yourself to help us understand who you are and what "silence" means to you. And thank you that, in that silence, you have helped me to "hear" you and many others more clearly. Please forgive us for our own stubborn deafness and persistent blindness and our dismal failure to accept deaf people as people.'

She had the energy to involve herself in a variety of different events — from charity functions, to visiting schools with deaf pupils, to conducting theatre workshops for deaf actors, to attending a Foyles Literary Lunch. She even spoke at the House of Commons, albeit in a reception room, where she joined the deaf MP Jack Ashley to launch a guide book to deaf organisations published by the Charities Aid Foundation. The only shade of disappointment arose from the confusion in some people's minds when they could not clearly separate the actress and the role. Some mistakenly thought that the silent defiance of Sarah Norman belonged equally to Elizabeth and failed to appreciate their different circumstances, that Elizabeth had a voice to use whereas Sarah Norman was not vocally equipped for speech and she (Sarah) knew it. Some others took it that Elizabeth was just another particularly good actress who in their opinion was not deaf at all. Both attitudes led to difficulties when theatregoers asked to meet her in her dressing room after the performance, as they regularly did. Elizabeth, who had spent much of her early life as an adoring fan of others, took trouble to make those meetings go smoothly:

> People would come to see me but when they arrived they were speechless. I had to realize that I had made an impact on them in the play and that they were as star-struck as I had been before, though I did not think I had done anything to earn it. You really have to be at the pinnacle of your career before you deserve that sort of treatment. So I learned that I had to help them, to go towards them. They all had their individual problems and they would talk to me about themselves which was better than platitudes about how marvellous I was. If they were prepared to share their thoughts and feelings with me I felt good about it. They would write and tell me how I had helped them with their own lives. I began to understand how you can help people by listening to them.

Others too shy to present themselves at her dressing room would send flowers or their own poems. There were less welcome attentions from strangers who waited around the stage door then followed her, but a burly carpenter from the theatre volunteered to escort her to her car when necessary. Outside the theatre, taxi drivers with their omniscient knowledge of London would recognise and befriend her and waiters in theatreland restaurants made sure she never lacked for service. Conversely, shop assistants who did not recognise her never guessed that she was deaf unless they turned their heads away and Elizabeth had to ask them to turn back so that she could read their lips.

Elizabeth read of an operation called a cochlear implant which was reputed to have dramatic effects in recovering hearing in the deaf. She went for a consultation with a Harley Street specialist recommended by Dr Latto, who told her that the operation had only proved successful with hard-of-hearing patients and even then it only had a one-in-five success rate. He still, however, asked to test her hearing. The last time Elizabeth had taken such a test had been in Austin, Texas, and it had taken a bottle of wine to console her when the definitively negative result came through. She resisted the idea of repeating the exercise but submitted eventually in the face of the specialist's insistence. After extensive tests on three different machines he could find no residual hearing. The result was what Elizabeth had expected and she took it calmly. The specialist was astonished at her mastery of speech without any hearing. She was still working on her voice and for six months went to a drama voice coach to improve her diction.

When the Society of West End Theatre awards ceremony came round again Elizabeth was invited to open one of the envelopes and make a presentation speech. Her mother had returned for a holiday with her and the two went to the awards dinner escorted by Richard O'Callaghan. The award was for best director and it had been won by Richard Eyre for his production of *Guys and Dolls* at the National Theatre. Elizabeth went on stage and, in a bold and confident voice, told the audience: 'The award you gave me last year has given me the confidence to speak to you tonight. We all know the importance of directors and the winner is ... ' Elizabeth then cunningly signed the name of Richard Eyre before verbally pronouncing it. She was rewarded with an approving round of applause, a compliment on her speech from Peter Ustinov who had also been making a presentation and warm letters of thanks from Mr

Eyre and the president of the Society. It was the first time her mother had heard her speak in public.

Richard O'Callaghan had become a permanent fixture in Elizabeth's life and a welcome one. He said: 'Obviously she is beautiful but she is so intelligent and courageous. I thought it was staggeringly brave of her to leave her family and loved ones and come over here where she knew no-one to tackle a major role like she has. It would be frightening enough for a hearing person. I admire her search for truth. She always wants criticism so that she can improve. She does not become defensive like the rest of us. It's a very mature view of life she has. She is not a starry person. She just wants to do her job as well and as truthfully as she can. When we are together we usually laugh a lot. We have the same sense of humour. It's strange. I never really think of her as being deaf.'

> I owe Richard a lot. He treats me as though there is nothing wrong with me. He treats me as a hearing friend. He sees me as a winner. He is very understanding and he makes me laugh a lot. He has a very good attitude to life. He is always simplifying things and I like that.

When Oliver Cotton's time to leave the show came round Elizabeth determined to make it a special performance. She committed every ounce of energy and inspiration to playing Sarah Norman that night and midway through the show Cotton signed to her: 'You are terrific.' It was the best performance they ever gave together. When Oliver Cotton left, in Spring 1983, his understudy Ron Aldridge was promoted to see out the rest of the run as the production entered its final stretch at the Albery.

Now there was interest in Elizabeth from other directions as the first approaches were made to see if she would undertake a spoken role on stage. First she was asked to combine a lunchtime fringe-theatre series of performances with *Children* but, though the more intimate space of the smaller theatre might have suited her for her first spoken role, she was not convinced that the play was right. Then she was contacted by a well-known producer who told her a play was being written specifically with her in mind. An established writer had seen her on 'Nationwide' and had prepared a synopsis of the play. Elizabeth expressed interest and the writer went off to work on his script.

Elizabeth played Sarah Norman in *Children of a Lesser God* for two years in London, an almost unprecedented run by a single actress in such a demanding role. As the London show came to its end there were the prospects of a British provincial tour of the play and also a tour of Australia:

> The difficulty with playing one role for a long time is that the emotional route map you create for yourself in the beginning to steer the character through each moment and convey the correct feelings to the audience does not last. Any emotion fades in time, even grief, so you have to find a new thought, a new stimulus, to trigger off the feeling you need. It is important for me that the audience share my journey through the play and the only way I can produce the effect I want is to feel the emotions of each moment as if I was experiencing them for the first time. I like acting to be very real, as near to life as possible. I like to feel that I do not know what is going to happen next and I think the best way to do that is by instinct and by using your imagination. The rapport with the audience is vital to me. I cannot hear them so I need to reach out and feel them. I know a lot of the time whether they are shifting in their seats or whispering because I can feel the vibrations. There has never been a character that I've felt as strongly about as Sarah Norman Leeds.

The goal of taking speaking roles on stage, if and when it happens, may be achieved only at some cost to Elizabeth as elements in the deaf community will take it as an act of disloyalty and rejection of them. Mel Carter, an American deaf friend of Elizabeth's, has a vast knowledge of the deaf world from his position as head of communications in the National Association of the Deaf in the United States. In his opinion:'She won't lose her real friends but there will be deaf people who will say she is a snobbish person and that she is snubbing the deaf world. Have you heard of the crab principle? When one crab

tries to climb out of the basket the other crabs try to pull him back. I am afraid that does happen in the deaf community. In fact, it happens in most minorities. It is often the case that when the oppressed get the chance they become the oppressor. I don't know how open the theatre is to someone like Liz making that move but if she does she is going to need all her strength and power and all the friends she can get. You really need a strong support group round you to try something like that.'
Richard O'Callaghan, with his knowledge of the theatre, takes a different view: 'I know there is a kind of envy among the militant deaf people. I believe in integrating rather than separating and that we should all mix together. Personally, I think Liz has such a special quality on stage that anyone who has a chance of using her in a spoken role would be mad to pass it up.'

Clarence Russell, the Spectrum leader from Texas, who was among the first to recognise Elizabeth's talent and who followed her career and her progress in *Children* from New York to London, sees other issues at stake in Elizabeth pursuing a vocal career in the theatre. He said: 'I do encourage Liz to try out for more roles, even though they require her to use voice only. It will enrich her experience and give her the opportunity to continue her acting career — for there are very, very limited and few roles for a sign language actor. But I would encourage [her] that it would be less noticeable or upsetting to the deaf community if she did her voice roles for hearing audiences only — with the understanding that she would probably not be patronised by the deaf audience. The reason for my thinking this way is that if you look at Helen Keller, she gave false hopes to parents of deaf/blind children. Not all can be as skilled as Helen Keller. I am afraid that with Liz's skill of speech in public places, namely theatres, she would give false hopes to hearing parents of deaf children. Liz would forever have to explain to the deaf why she did it. The deaf community would think she was ashamed of being deaf and that was why she would rather do hearing roles. It would destroy a wonderful part of Liz's skill of acting, because she would spend more time explaining why she accepted hearing roles instead of explaining how she became an actress.'

While Elizabeth's future remains unknown the progress and development of her past is worthy of celebration and she has no more ardent champion than the Broadway producer Manny Azenberg, who was so determined to place her centre-stage in London: 'When Liz went over to London for the previews she was crazy, disjointed and really going through a colossal insecurity. I told her she was about to start on one of the great experiences of her life and if she did not enjoy it then it would purely be her own fault. It was so obvious that here was a girl who was going to do wonderfully but if she got too frightened and could not enjoy it then she was doomed. No-one could anticipate that the world would open up to her the way it did. It was glorious, and just to be peripherally attached to providing that experience for someone else, well, it was great for me. As far as I can see she has survived the entry into the hearing world. After *Children* she will have a fuller life and broader horizons and be able to deal with the rest of her life. She once asked me if she could be a speaking actress. I said I didn't know. There would always be a problem. Would she have the technique of vocal control? Could she make it? As an actress she will be limited by her deafness. It is going to preclude certain things. She is going to be handicapped, she's going to be up against Maggie Smith and Diane Keaton, you can't get past that. In terms of being a human being she is not handicapped at all. Quite the opposite. Maybe she knows more than any of us because she knows what it is like to be different. I can't claim that I've been involved in or responsible for the growth she has undergone. People do it for themselves.

'Hell, it's one of the best stories I know and it's not over yet.'

Epilogue

More than twenty years ago I read a poem by Robert Frost. It was called 'The Road Not Taken'. I was a schoolgirl when I read it, barely ten years old, yet that poem has always stayed with me. It describes the choice of two paths which a traveller is faced with in a wood, and it ends:

I took the one less travelled by
And that has made all the difference.

Looking back over the intervening years, that poem seems unexpectedly true of my own journey. I could have spent my life in the safety of the deaf world (although I felt I was only partly a member of that society), or I could have taken my chance in the hearing world. Instead I chose to become an actress, which is a hard enough profession even if you have hearing. There were problems, there were times of pain and there were times when I felt like giving up; but to have given up would have meant to betray the one thing that I was sure of, that the stage was where I belonged.

We are all the product of our experiences and if I had taken a different course I would not be the person I am. I am pleased to be where I am today. I believe I am a much fuller person because of what has happened to me, but I realize that I still have a long way to go. I know that I have been fortunate and there are many things I am grateful for, including friends who have helped me to see that a problem which seems like the end of the world at first glance can look downright ridiculous when you get it into perspective; but most of all I am aware that I was blessed with an exceptional family. Whatever I do in my life, I think that nothing will make me as proud as the knowledge that I am the daughter of Jack and Anita Quinn.

In a way I feel I have paid my dues. It was a long road and a hard road and, quite honestly, I would not want to do it again. It had to be done, but once was enough.

What kept me going? However bad things became, there was always some nugget of instinct inside me pushing me on. Even when my insecurity was at its worst, when I was leaving America or going through the rehearsals at the Mermaid, there was something inside me which told me I was doing the right thing. I did not always have the confidence to listen to it. I tried different jobs in the hearing world and they did not seem right for me. I tried the deaf world in Chicago and at Spectrum, but that did not seem right either. I believed that my place was on the stage and that belief slowly grew, but it was not until the first night of *Children of a Lesser God* in London that I absolutely knew I was right. Whatever strength I had had must have been in my subconscious but that night it came to the surface. There was also the advice my father gave me, to take one day at a time and see what that day brings. The frustration I had felt through most of my life of not being able to express my personality, of being held back from developing and not being part of the wider world, also built up until it became a positive force urging me on.

Another factor, and part of the reason why I chose to be an actress — which was just about the hardest thing I could aim for — was a need to communicate. It is something all artists have and in my case it takes the form of being able to express ideas and emotions to an audience and to touch them and affect their lives. It is by sharing our knowledge and experience that we all learn. I do not believe that acting is about entertaining people. Acting is *being* there, being loyal to the character you are playing and trying to do that character justice. It is about being honest and having the courage to open up and let people see exactly what you are thinking and feeling at every moment of the play. In that way the performance becomes a shared experience between the actor and the audience.

Watching some of the finest actors performing in films or on stage, I am always impressed with the way they use silence. Without saying a word, they can convey their feelings to the audience through their bodies and their faces. Very often words are not as important as the visual image. And when great actors bring something magical to a role, I think it has to do with the simplicity of their performance. There is great strength in simplicity — especially in silence.

On and off stage I watch people all the time, studying their expressions and their gestures because I like to know what is going on behind the words people say. Billy taught me to do that. He watches people very, very closely and although I am not nearly as perceptive as he is, I am working on it. Maybe, off stage, people are frightened of silence. They feel they have to say something, even if it amounts to nothing. Silence is more effective. If someone says something and instead of replying you just look at them, that is more powerful than words. They can see all that you feel in your face. If there has to be a word, it should come afterwards, like a full stop.

One of the hardest lessons I have had to learn is that of discipline. I never really had any formal study or training. At school I was too restless, at college I was rebellious and I never went to acting school, so I have had to find my own discipline and that takes a long time. The other big break was getting out of the dependence on others which I had felt all my life. For too long I had had people taking care of me — from family, friends and teachers to theater directors. The result was that my development as an adult was delayed. I was going through experiences in my twenties which other girls go through in their teens. It was embarrassing. Now I have learned to stand on my own and, if I do fall down, I know how to get up again. I have learned to be tough and to handle my own problems. I am coming out of my dream world and learning to be more realistic. There is nothing I dislike more than being pampered or babied. I have finally allowed the woman in me to emerge — that part of myself which I resisted for so long.

Perhaps the latest and most welcome thing that has happened

to me is that for the first time I have a sense of optimism. I feel ready for the future, whatever it holds. I am ready for change. In the old days any change was a great disturbance and a cause of anxiety. I always felt that I was being uprooted from something which had become safe and familiar and being plunged into the dangerous unknown. Now I am ready to dive right in off the high board.

My father told me that I would find my own faith in my own time. I am not sure that I have found it yet, but I do believe that there is a purpose behind everything that happens and, believing that, it is easier to accept what comes along and to use each experience as a chance to grow.

In my own case, my response to the sea is perhaps the closest I have come to a religious experience. The sea is never still, it is restless, it can be wild, it is different from day to day and it has moods of its own. It was by the sea that my dreams first started; in times of distress it was the sea which provided comfort and solace, restored and rejuvenated me. Inside, I am still that little girl on the beach, running and laughing with Billy. I will always carry with me the space, the freedom and the laughter. I love to laugh.

I do not believe that my journey has been all that exceptional, or that I have done all I have alone. But, as Robert Frost said:

> *Two roads diverged in a wood, and I —*
> *I took the one less travelled by*
> *And that has made all the difference.*

Elizabeth Quinn
LONDON, 1983.